Anonymous

A Round Table of the Representative Irish and English Catholic Novelists

Anonymous

A Round Table of the Representative Irish and English Catholic Novelists

ISBN/EAN: 9783337039868

Printed in Europe, USA, Canada, Australia, Japan

Cover: Foto ©ninafisch / pixelio.de

More available books at **www.hansebooks.com**

Louisa Emily Dobrée

M. E. Francis. Theo. Gift

Katharine Tynan Hinkson.

Pauline von Hügel
          C de la R

Amahl Keov

R. B. Sheridan Knowles

F. U. Maitland

Sophie Maude

Clara Mulholland

Rosa Mulholland Gilbert

Mrs Bartle Teeling

A ROUND TABLE

OF THE REPRESENTATIVE

IRISH AND ENGLISH CATHOLIC NOVELISTS,

AT WHICH IS SERVED A FEAST OF EXCELLENT STORIES

BY

LOUISA EMILY DOBRÉE, FRANCES M. MAITLAND,
M. E. FRANCIS, SOPHIE MAUDE,
THEO. GIFT, CLARA MULHOLLAND,
BARONESS PAULINE VON HÜGEL, ROSA MULHOLLAND,
LADY AMABEL KERR, MRS. BARTLE TEELING,
R. B. SHERIDAN KNOWLES, KATH. TYNAN HINKSON.

With Portraits, Biographical Sketches, and Bibliography.

THIRD EDITION.

NEW YORK, CINCINNATI, CHICAGO:
BENZIGER BROTHERS,

Contents.

		PAGE
A Dress Ring, ...	Louisa Emily Dobrée	9
In St. Patrick's Ward, ...	M. E. Francis	29
A Soldier's Wife, ...	Theo. Gift	51
Fair Dorothy Wilmot, .	Baroness Pauline von Hügel	49
Just What Was Wanted, . . .	Lady Amabel Kerr	105
Hyacinth's Regrets, ...	R. B. Sheridan Knowles	129
Miss Packe, ...	Frances M. Maitland	167
A Paste Buckle, ...	Sophie Maude	201
Mave's Repentance, ...	Clara Mulholland	225
Granny Grogan, ...	Rosa Mulholland Gilbert	249
Her Last Stake, ...	Mrs. Bartle Teeling	275
The Wardrobe, ...	Katharine Tynan Hinkson	323

LOUISA EMILY DOBRÉE.

LOUISA EMILY DOBRÉE, a native of Tours, France, is of Irish descent on her mother's side, while her father's family, which is a Guernsey one, was originally French, as the name shows.

Miss Dobrée's first story was published when she was nineteen. This was followed by fugitive articles and short stories in magazines as well as books for young people, among which are the following: "Loved into Shape," "Dreams and Deeds," "Terry," "One Talent Only," "A

Knotless Thread," "Underneath the Surface," "A Lowly Life with a Lofty Aim," and "Turned to Gold." These were published at intervals of sometimes great length.

In 1887 Miss Dobrée was received into the Catholic Church, and her books since then have been: "A Manual of Home Nursing," "Stories on the Sacraments," "A Seven-Fold Treasure," "Per Parcel Post," "A Tug-of-War," "Stories on the Beatitudes," "Beautiful Sewing," "Plain Work," etc. She is on the staff and an occasional contributor to twenty magazines, the subjects on which she writes including home nursing, domestic and personal hygiene, etiquette, character sketches, embroidery, plain work, natural history, etc.

Miss Dobrée has lived a great deal in the Channel Islands, France, and Ireland, besides having paid visits, long and short, to Italy, Switzerland, Austria, Belgium, Germany, etc. The scenes of her stories are constantly laid on the continent of Europe. She lives now, as she has done for the past nine years, at Chiswick, near London.

A Dress Ring.

BY LOUISA EMILY DOBRÉE.

In cockney parlance they had been keeping company and walking together for quite a year, so that when they by mutual agreement were to be formally engaged the bestowal of a ring was a sequence also decided upon. This ring is called a "dress ring," and as a rule it contains stones or their imitation of some kind or other, differing in this from the plain gold circle to which it is one day to be a companion, provided of course that the course of the engagement runs smoothly and terminates in marriage. "They" were two young people named severally Joe Smith and Victoria Harris. He was a tall, burly youth with better developed muscles and air of health than is usually seen in a London artisan, while she, a slight, small narrow-chested girl, had anæmia writ large on the dead white face, pallid lips, and shadowed eyes, the latter capable of various expressions gleaming under her "idiot's frill" of black hair, above which on this particular summer afternoon was set a huge hat adorned with a blue feather which had swallowed up a large part of her week's earnings.

They were on a bench in a London park; and the fact that his arm was not round her waist, or her head on his shoulder, due to Joe's inherent shyness and Victoria's native modesty, somewhat marked them off from the many other lovers who here and there were in confused heaps and stolid, unblushing faces on which those who ran might read careless indifference to the decorum of life. They were genuinely in love with each other, and as far as character went they were as unlike as in relative appearance. The little wisp of a girl, whose pert tongue and peppery temper often made her lover stare in astonishment, admired Joe's quiet, silent ways, and felt that he was a great and safe support to her. She could tell him all her troubles about her drunken father who had cast her, his only motherless child, off when she was fifteen and told her to look out for herself, and be sure of a kind, patient listener and one who would try to suggest some way of helping the man and who would not be too hard on him. This won Victoria's heart and gave Joe in time a large place in it, for the girl loved her very worthless parent with strange, unreasoning tenacity, and had her lover attempted to condemn him she would have turned like an angry cat upon him. And Joe liked Victoria's quickness, thought her smart speech very fetching, and her little bursts of temper glanced over him when he was not astonished at them.

"I do believe it's going to rine," said Victoria

presently, as the sky suddenly clouded over, and there was that stillness in the air broken by the twittering of birds which presages a summer shower, "and I haven't got no umbereller," and she thought with dismay of her hat and its fine curly feather.

"I don't expect it will be much, and we might get under that there tree, it's got a sight more leaves than this one 'as," said Joe, thinking that he also was umbrella-less and that his hat had been freshly ironed the day before.

"All right, let's get there then—come, look sharp," said Victoria, who was prompt in most things; and the two ran across to the other bench, which was well sheltered by a widely spreading tree from the heavy shower which came down then and there with no indecision.

Both had the same subject in their minds, and yet neither liked alluding to it. They each were thinking of that dress ring that lay in Joe's waistcoat pocket, the bestowal of which both knew was to take place that afternoon, and the occasion of the engagement of which it was a sign was at the back of the hat-ironing and purchase of the feather.

They were silent for a few minutes as the rain beat the leaves and a few drops penetrated the outer branches and fell on the sunburnt grass.

Joe coughed. He wished Victoria would refer to the subject, and she, perfectly aware of the fact and enjoying his silent shyness, was determined not to lead up to it in any way.

"Mrs. Parsons has been that cross this week, she've never stopped jawin' of us for one thing or another. My mate catched it Friday 'cause she scorched some of the finery—lor', wasn't the fat in the fire!" said Victoria, secretly unbuttoning her left-hand glove, which, of stiff kid, had cost one and sixpence three farthings, and were desperately uncomfortable.

"Were there? Oh—Vickey—I say."

"Yes?" said Vickey, looking, with blank innocence of what he wanted to say, into his honest but rather stupid blue eyes.

"I've got the ring, Vickey, and Father Wrighton blessed it all right," said Joe, coloring and speaking in a low tone of voice.

"Oh, have yer?" said Vickey. "Let's see it, then—do be quick, Joe," she added, for, now she was certain he had the ring, curiosity vanquished coquetry.

Joe fumbled with his big fingers in his waistcoat pocket, and then withdrew the little card box which he then handed to Vickey. There lying in the pink cotton was a ring with three blue stones in it. Vickey's quick tongue for a moment was silent, for she was altogether surprised, the ring being so very much better than that which her fancy painted Joe was likely to give her, and he, rising to the occasion, took it out of its soft nest, placed it on her finger and, park or no park, gave Vickey a sounding kiss as he did so.

"Glad you like it," said Joe, answering her unspoken approbation. "I picked it out from a lot—chose blue special, as you're partial to the color."

"Yus, it's my fav'rite color," said Vickey, who liked blue, not only for its own sake, but because it was Our Lady's color, and she was looking forward to being a Child of Mary some day. She had worn the aspirant's green ribbon for more than a year, and what it and the little medal had done for her in keeping her from dangerous paths, in checking that fiery temper of hers, in fortifying her against the hundred or more temptations that crowd round the rough life of a laundry girl, she and her guardian angels best knew.

"It's a beauty," said Vickey; "must ha' cost a lot."

Joe looked rather sheepish.

"Oh, well, I ain't stony broke yet along of it, nor I haven't 'ad to go and see my uncle. Now, Vickey, you'll kipe it on noight and dye until I puts on the plain gold 'un, eh?"

"Well, you are a Sawney! Just to think o' me a-washin' and a-scrubbin' with that lovely ring on! Where'd the blue jools be, I'd like to know, if I did? I reckon they'd be lost in the soap-suds in no time if so be as the ring didn't take itself off altogether and go down the wyste-water poipes. I'll put it on a Sundays and when I gets out."

"Well, you must do as you loike," said Joe.

"That's about my ticket generally," said Vickey coolly, and Joe knew that was true as far as trifles went.

"I picked you out a nice one, now didn't I?"

"Yes. I'm deloighted with it."

"Now there's something else as I've got to——"

"Give me!" exclaimed Vickey, wondering if Joe had added to his gift by the purchase of a brooch or bangle.

"Well, not to give you, unless telling you news is giving."

"Do come out with it, then, quick."

"It's like this, Vickey. I my 'ave a roise about Christmas toime. The guv'nor was 'intin' at it and chaffin' me a bit about 'avin' a young lydy and thinkin' o' settlin' down. We'd rub along pretty fair on the pye I'd 'ave then."

Vickey was silent. She was stirred to the depths by his words. Marriage had been, of course, in her mind now and then, but that it might be so near and Joe her very own "for better for worse, for richer for poorer"—nothing but death to part them! All the "eternal-womanly" shone in Vickey's face and was the key to the slightly quivering lips, the soft gentle tone in which she answered at length, "Where 'ud we live?"

It sounded a commonplace, matter-of-fact question, but Vickey had known no home since the day that her father had sold the furniture over her head and turned her literally out of doors, and one trembles to think what might have become of her had not Mrs. Parsons, the owner of the laundry where she worked by the day, taken her in and made her live there. In her rough way she had been kind to her, but a home of her own—Vickey knew that would be a very different thing.

"There's a nice little flat in the models," said Joe, alluding to some model lodging-houses recently built. "You know the ones I mean by the stytion."

Vickey nodded.

"It would be dreadfully nice, Joe."

"You'd marry me, then, supposin' I gits the roise?" inquired Joe, who sometimes felt as if he was not quite sure of Vickey.

"Yus."

They lingered a while in the park, and the rain was followed by sunshine and a lovely sky. Then they sauntered on towards Ansmith, the suburb in which Vickey lived, and reached the church while the bell still clanged.

Joe sang in the choir, and to Vickey his untrained and somewhat gruff bass was like a voice from heaven, so beautiful did it sound to her. Perhaps to the angelic choir, who knew it was the singing of a rough artisan who amid the temptations of the world was trying as he best knew how to live the clean straight life of a good Catholic, the harsh tones had music in them!

On Monday there was not much to be done in the laundry. As a rule, Vickey went in the van to collect the clothes, but that day another girl went; she simply helped a little in odd ways and did not set to work until three o'clock, when the girls and women who did not live there came.

Vickey and the girl who was her special mate were having tea together in the sorting-room, the rest of the workers being in the ironing-room.

Vickey, needless to say, was burning to show her new possession to Tilda, and the latter, when she heard that Vickey had it, was naturally very curious to see it.

"Ain't it lovely?" said Vickey, slipping it out, then holding out her hand to show it off.

Tilda looked at it critically.

"It don't look as good as the one Bill give me."

"It's a very good one," said Vickey, withdrawing her hand hurriedly. "Anyway I'm pleased with it."

"Tyke it off and let me see it better," said Tilda, and Vickey drew it off.

"What are yer lookin' at?" asked Vickey, for Tilda was not looking at the lovely stones, but was peering inside the ring.

"No, I thought it worn't," said Tilda, in a satisfied tone of voice. "It's not a bit more than noine carat gold."

"What's carrots got to do with it?" asked Vickey, rather mystified.

"It's something as says how good the gold is," said Tilda. "Bill's father's in the joollery tride, and he knows all about it. The one he give me was eighteen carat gold, just double as good as this here. Well, I'm sorry for yer, Vickey, for if your chap don't care for you enough to give yer a good ring, I say he oughter be ashamed of hisself. It's downright mean, I call it. Can't you see the noine?"

Vickey silently took the ring, held it up to the light and saw the figure clearly enough. To her eyes, gleaming now with annoyance she was trying to hide, the ring had lost all its beauty, and she felt humiliated and made to appear very small in Tilda's eyes. However, she said nothing, and did not even defend Joe from the imputation of not caring for her, and as the work-bell rung at that minute to announce the expiration of the tea-hour, all further discussion was stopped.

After work was over Vickey ran round to a little jeweller's close by, had the ring tested, and found that her last hope—which was that Tilda might be mistaken as to the relative value of the nine or eighteen—was wrong. The ring had been a very cheap one indeed, and worth a few shillings at the outside.

Tilda attempted a renewal of the subject in vain. Vickey would not speak of it, and through the week she fumed and fretted inwardly to such a degree that she made herself thoroughly miserable. With her imagination excited by anger, she saw significance in many things Joe had said and done, all tending, she now firmly believed, to prove that he did not care enough for her to think her worth a good ring, these bitter reflections completely effacing all other things which showed that she had no reason to doubt his affection.

It was a wretched week. Vickey made mistakes in the sorting, scorched a baby's frock, and finally broke the marble slab on which the shirt-fronts were ironed and brought up to the regulation pitch of shininess. These things had not a tranquillizing effect on Vickey's temper, and on her evening out she got a line from Joe to say he could not come and see her as usual. That was the last straw.

At last the long week came to an end, and as it poured with rain on Sunday afternoon, there was no thought of going out, and Joe came prepared for a pleasant time indoors.

The two could have the parlor to themselves, as Mrs. Parsons, who was tired, was lying down in her room and was likely to be there until tea-time.

It was a small prim room with a coo table, in the centre of which were wax flowers under a glass case which reposed on a crochet mat. There was a large oil painting of the late Mr. Parsons on the wall, flanked by a double row of family photographs, and on the chimney were shells and memorial cards of various kinds.

"Bloomin', I 'ope, Vickey," said Joe, as he entered the room where Vickey was seated in a stiff horsehair-covered chair.

Vickey did not answer, and Joe did not venture on more than a handshake, which on Vickey's side was limp.

"This 'ere's for you," said Vickey, coming to the point at once and handing Joe the box.

"Why, Vickey—whatever's up?"

"Whatever's up, indeed! Like your cheek givin' me a ring what ain't worth 'avin' and hardly gold at all! If I ain't worth a good ring I won't have one at all."

Joe colored.

"'Ow do ye know it ain't good? Who said so?"

"I says so. And I went and 'ad it seen at a jooller's. Yes, it's gold, he says, says he, but the poorest kind almost as there is."

"So you doubted of me, and cared only for the vallyer of the ring," said Joe, who, seldom stirred, could be angry once in a way. "Yer a nice one, I must sye."

"Can't return the compliment," said Vickey coolly. "I don't know 'ow ye dared give me such a bit o' rubbish."

"'Tain't rubbish," said Joe shortly. "It mayn't be what you may call a fust-clarse ring, but it was as good as I could get ye, and if you 'ad cared fur me you wouldn't have thought about it," and Joe shut the cardboard cover down on the poor little ring.

Vickey bit her lips.

"There's explinyshuns as I could give you just to show you——" began Joe.

"I don't want non' o' yer explinyshuns—very likely I didn't care," and Vickey shot a withering glance in Joe's direction. At it Joe felt as if he grew suddenly cold, and he repented of his momentary anger, now that there was no mistake about Vickey's serious displeasure.

"No," exclaimed Vickey, "no, I don't want ter 'ear anything you may have to sye. You've treated me shimeful. I know now why you didn't want me to take it off night nor dye, and——"

"Do let me speak," said Joe, who now was all too anxious to talk.

"I ain't a fool. When we've been keepin' company all this while for you to give me that ring, 'ardly gold at all, but faked up with some stuff they calls carrots, is a downright insult, when you've drawed money out of the savings bank—a fi'-pun note, too!"

Joe stared from sheer astonishment.

"Yes, my mate was at the post-office the other dye and just behind you when you got the money out. So it wasn't as you 'adn't it."

"If you'd——"

"No, I shan't. You don't come no tiles over me," said Vickey, working herself up more and more, until she was in such a fury that Joe saw any attempt at getting a hearing was futile. Although he thought and acted slowly, he made up his mind that he would come again when she had cooled down and tell her—well, what might turn the tables very considerably.

"You go off this minute. Get another young lydy when you like," said Vickey. "I don't never wish to see you agine!" So saying, she drew herself up and tried to look all injured innocence as she ran out of the room. And throwing herself on her bed, she sobbed her heart and her temper out.

If the preceding week had been unsatisfactory, this one promised to be worse, and after the little sleep gained after sleepless hours, Vickey woke to the reality of her misery. All the morning she could think of nothing else but what had happened, and she went about with a very white face. Her companions, seeing that she was unhappy and finding that she would not reveal the cause, left her alone.

She wondered if Joe would really take her at her word, or if he would come as usual on Thursday, which was early-closing day for him, and it seemed to her as if that day was years instead of but a few days distant. Although she was still extremely angry with Joe, the tempest had so far passed that she was able to hear the whispers of conscience and common sense. Both said the same to her, namely, that she had been wrong to make such a fuss, still more foolish to quarrel absolutely about it, and unfair to Joe not to listen to his explanations. Then, too, she remembered with unpleasant distinctness how very good he had always been to her, how patient with her peppery temper, how forbearing with her sharp words. They had had a tiff or two ere now, but this was the most serious of all, and by dinner-time Vickey in her secret soul began to hope that Joe was not such a fool as to think she really meant to throw him up.

In the late afternoon Mrs. Parsons wanted some soap-jelly, and sent Vickey for it. As the girl walked along, her thoughts were still so busy that she did not notice much where she was going, and as she turned a corner ran right against a man.

" 'Ollo, Vickey ! "

" Well, I never—father ! "

" Yes, it's me," said Mr. Harris. " I was goin' round to yer plice to give you a call."

" Well, I never ! " exclaimed Vickey, looking her father up and down and wondering if the decently clad man could be he. " You are a toff ! "

Harris drew himself up. He had had a shave quite recently, his hair was well brushed, his clothes clean and orderly, and altogether he looked very different indeed from the sodden-faced, blear-eyed individual she had last seen three months back who had come whining to her for money to spend at the Three Feathers.

"Yes," said Harris, pleased at the effect his appearance was making on Vickey, "I've gone up a step or two, 'aven't I?"

Vickey's face was irradiated with a smile. She loved her father dearly in spite of all, and this transformation filled her heart with joy.

"It's all along o' your chap," said Harris, turning and walking with Vickey. "Wot d' yer think he done? Well, he's bin a-coming after me ever since I last seen yer, a-persuadin' o' me to turn over a new leaf, as the sayin' is. He's a perseverin' chap, I must say, is Joe, an' lawst week he hears of a situytion for me and he gets me these 'ere clothes and fitted me out in this style."

"And why didn't I know on this?" asked Vickey quickly.

"Well, it was his secret, so to speak. Says he, 'Don't let on to Vickey till you've made a real good start and mean to stick to it. She won't believe of it unless you do.' He's one of the right sort, is Joe, and he an' me is very chummy now, and I think, my girl, as you've done very well for yourself in gittin' 'im. We'd got it all arranged, as I was to call and surprise yer."

"Well, you've done that," was all Vickey found to say, and after a little more talk they parted at the laundry door.

Vickey hardly knew how to think collectedly, and as the tea-bell rang she ran up to her room, her brain full of bewildering thoughts, her heart rejoicing over her father, and aching with remorse about Joe all the same.

"Hextry speshul! Piper! Evenin' piper! Terrible accident on the —— London line. List of killed and injured."

The shrill voices of the paper boys fell on her ears, and in a minute more she had secured a paper. It had rushed suddenly to her recollection that it was on Joe's line of work the accident had occurred. With trembling hands she turned over the pages, and among the injured was "J. Smith."

Vickey never knew how she accomplished that journey, really a short one, but apparently interminable to her. She had all the quickness of the born cockney, the familiarity with ways and means of getting about, due to having had to look out for herself from early years and being continually employed as messenger for Mrs. Parsons.

At last she reached the hospital where the injured had been taken, and the busy porter told her she certainly might go up to Alexandra ward and ask to see No. 15.

So Vickey went up the wide stone staircases and along the lofty corridor, conscious of the strong odor of carbolic acid, the students clattering down with note-books, the white-capped nurses. There was no difficulty about being admitted, and Vickey walked down the ward with its speckless sand-covered boards, its rows of blue-quilted beds, its white stoves on which were palms and flowers. The long windows showed the tops of many roofs, countless chimney-pots, a few spires, and above all the burning, fiery glow of the sunset, the opal lights, the unearthly colors.

Vickey drew back and clutched the nurse's arm as the latter stopped before a screen, which told its own tale.

"Is he so bad as that?" she whispered, and the nurse looked at her compassionately.

Before she could speak Vickey's quick ear caught the words spoken in low reverent tones by the priest behind the screen:

"*Requiem æternam dona ei Domine!*"

M. E. FRANCIS.

Mrs. Frances Blundell (M. E. Francis) is the second daughter of the late Michael James Sweetman, of Lamberton Park, Queen's County, Ireland. Her mother was the only daughter and heiress of Michael Powell, of Fitzwilliam Square, Dublin, and Richview, County Dublin. Miss Sweetman was born at Killiney Park, County Dublin, brought up at Lamberton Park, and married, in 1879, Francis Nicholas Blundell, who died in 1884.

After her marriage she lived entirely at Crosby, Lancashire, the scene of the " North Country Village," which is, perhaps, her best known book.

One of her sisters is Mrs. Egerton Castle, wife of the well-known *littérateur*. Another is Miss Elinor Sweetman, whose " Palms," and fugitive pieces, have been singled out by the press for favorable notice.

Miss Sweetman's first printed tale was written when she was fourteen, and secured the distinction of being published through the interest of the Rev. Matthew Russell, S.J., editor of *The Irish Monthly*, in which journal a more mature effort appeared in November, 1879. Her first long story, " Molly's Fortunes," appeared in *The Irish Monthly*, and has since been followed by many others, chiefly sketches of Irish village life. " Whither ? " her first three-volume novel, was published in 1892, followed after an interval of six months by " In a North Country Village." In the spring of 1894 the " Story of Dan " appeared. This is a romance of Irish peasant life, and both scenes and characters were well known to the author in her childhood.

That same year " A Daughter of the Soil " had the honor of being selected as the first serial which was to appear in the weekly edition of *The Times*, and was afterwards published in book form. Since then she has published " Frieze and Fustian," a collection of sketches of peasant life in Ireland and Lancashire, and various short stories, most of which are shortly to be re-issued in volume form, under the title of " Among the Untrodden Ways."

In St. Patrick's Ward.

BY M. E. FRANCIS.

It was intensely, suffocatingly hot, though the windows on either side of the long room were wide open; the patients lay languidly watching the flies on the ceiling, the sunshine streaming over the ochre-tinted wall, the flickering light of the little lamp which burned night and day beneath the large colored statue of St. Patrick in the centre of the ward. It was too hot even to talk. Granny M'Gee—who, though not exactly ill, was old and delicate enough to be permitted to remain permanently in the Union Infirmary instead of being relegated to the workhouse proper—dozed in her wicker-chair with her empty pipe between her wrinkled fingers. Once, as she loved to relate, she had burnt her lovely fringe with that same pipe—" bad luck to it ! " but she invariably hastened to add that her heart 'ud be broke out an' out if it wasn't for the taste o' baccy. Her neighbor opposite was equally fond of snuff, and was usually to be heard lamenting how she had rared a fine fam'ly o' boys an' girls and how notwithstanding she had ne'er a wan to buy her a ha'porth in her ould age. Now, however, for a wonder she was silent, and even the woman nearest the door found it too hot to brandish her distorted wrists according to her custom when she wished to excite compassion or to plead for alms. There would be no visitors this morning; not the most compassionate of "the ladies," who came to read and otherwise cheer the poor sufferers of St. Patrick's ward, would venture there on such a day.

The buzzing of the flies aforesaid, the occasional moans of the more feeble patients, the hurried breathing of a poor girl in the last stage of consumption were the only sounds to be heard, except for the quiet footsteps and gentle voice of Sister Louise. There was something refreshing in the very sight of this tall slight figure, in its blue-gray habit and dazzling white "cornette" from beneath which the dark eyes looked forth with sweet and almost childish directness. Sister Louise was not indeed much more than a child in years, and there were still certain inflections in her voice, an elasticity in her movements, a something about her very hands, with their little pink palms and dimpled knuckles, that betrayed the fact. But those babyish hands had done good service since Sister Louise had left the novitiate in the Rue du Bac two years before; that young voice had a marvellous power of its own, and could exhort and reprove as well as soothe and console; and when the blue-robed figure was seen flitting up and down the ward smiles appeared on wan and sorrowful faces, and querulous murmurs were hushed. Even to-day the patients nodded to her languidly as she passed, observing with transitory cheerfulness that they were kilt with the hate, or that it was terrible weather entirely. One crone roused herself sufficiently to remark that it was a fine thing for the counthry, glory be to God! which patriotic sentiment won a smile from Sister Louise, but failed to awaken much enthusiasm in any one else.

The Sister of Charity paused before a bed in which a little, very thin old woman was coiled up with eyes half closed. Mrs. Brady was the latest arrival at St. Patrick's ward, having indeed only "come in" on the preceding day; and Sister Louise thought she would very likely need a little cheering.

"How are you to-day, Mrs. Brady?" she asked, bending over her.

"Why then indeed, ma'am—is it ma'am or mother I ought to call ye?"

"'Sister'—we are all Sisters here, though some of the people call Sister Superior 'Reverend Mother.'"

"Ah, that indeed?" said Mrs. Brady, raising herself a little in the bed, and speaking with great dignity. "Ye see yous are not the sort o' nuns I'm used to, so you'll excuse me if I don't altogether spake the way I ought. Our nuns down in the Queen's County has black veils, ye know, ma'am—Sisther, I mane—an' not that kind of a white bonnet that you have on your head."

"Well, do you know our patients here get quite fond of our white wings, as they call them," returned Sister Louise, smiling. "But you haven't told me how you are, yet. Better I hope, and pretty comfortable."

A tear suddenly rolled down Mrs. Brady's cheek, but she preserved her lofty manner.

"Ah, yes, thank ye, Sisther, as comfortable as I could expect in a place like this. Of course I niver thought it's here I'd be, but it's on'y for a short time, thanks be to God! My little boy'll be comin' home from America soon to take me out of it."

"Why, that's good news!" cried the Sister cheerfully. "We must make you quite well and strong—that is, as strong as we can"—with a compassionate glance, "by the time he comes. When do you expect him?"

"Any day now, ma'am—Sisther, I mane—aye, indeed, I may say any day an' every day, an' I'm afeard his heart'll be broke findin' me in this place. But no matther!"

Here she shook her head darkly, as though she could say much on that subject, but refrained out of consideration for Sister Louise.

"Well, we must do all we can for you meanwhile," said the latter gently. "Have you made acquaintance with your neighbors yet? Poor Mrs.

M'Evoy here is worse off than you, for she can't lift her head just now. Tell Mrs. Brady how it was you hurt your back, Mrs. M'Evoy."

"Bedad, Sisther, ye know yerself it was into the canal I fell wid a can o' milk," said the old woman addressed, squinting fearfully in her efforts to catch a glimpse of the new patient. "The Bishop says the last time he come round, 'I s'pose,' he says, 'ye were goin' to put wather in the milk.' 'No,' says I, 'there was wather enough in it before.'"

Here Mrs. M'Evoy leered gleefully up at the Sister, and one or two feeble chuckles were heard from the neighboring beds; but Mrs. Brady assumed an attitude which can only be described as one implying a mental drawing away of skirts, and preserved an impenetrable gravity. Evidently she had never associated with "the like" of Mrs. M'Evoy in the circles in which she had hitherto moved.

"And there's Kate Mahony on the other side," pursued Sister Louise, without appearing to notice Mrs. Brady's demeanor. "She has been lying here for seventeen years, haven't you, Kate?"

"Aye, Sisther," said Kate, a thin-faced, sweet-looking woman of about forty, looking up brightly.

"Poor Kate!" said the Sister, in a caressing tone. "You must get Kate to tell you her story some time, Mrs. Brady. She has seen better days like you."

"Oh, that indeed?" said Mrs. Brady, distantly but politely, and with a dawning interest, "I s'pose you are from the country then, like meself."

"Ah, no, ma'am," returned Kate. "I may say I was never three miles away from town. I went into service when I was on'y a slip of a little girl, an' lived with the wan lady till the rheumatic fever took me, an' made me what I am now. You're not from this town, I s'pose, ma'am."

"Indeed, I'd be long sorry to come from such a dirty place—beggin' your pardon for sayin' it. No, indeed, I am from the Queen's County, near Mar'boro'. We had the loveliest little farm there ye could see, me an' me poor husband, the Lord ha' mercy on his soul! Aye, indeed, it's little we ever thought—but no matther! Glory be to goodness! my little boy'll be comin' back from America soon to take me out o' this."

"Sure it's well for ye," said Kate, "that has a fine son o' your own to work for ye. Look at me without a crature in the wide world belongin' to me! An' how long is your son in America, ma'am?"

"Goin' on two year, now," said Mrs. Brady, with a sigh.

"He'll be apt to be writin' to ye often, I s'pose, ma'am."

"Why then, indeed, not so often. The poor fellow he was niver much of a hand at the pen.

He's movin' about, ye see, gettin' work here an' there."

Sister Louise had moved on, seeing that the pair were likely to make friends; and before ten minutes had elapsed each was in possession of the other's history. Kate's, indeed, was simple enough; her seventeen years in the infirmary being preceded by a quiet life in a very uninteresting neighborhood; but she "came of decent people," being connected with "the rale ould O'Rorkes," and her father had been "in business"—two circumstances which impressed Mrs. Brady very much, and caused her to unbend towards "Miss Mahony," as she now respectfully called her new acquaintance. The latter was loud in expressions of admiration and sympathy as Mrs. Brady described the splendors of the past; the servant-man and her servant-maid who, according to her, once formed portion of her establishment; the four beautiful milch-cows which her husband kept, besides sheep, and a horse and car, and "bastes" innumerable; the three little b'yes they buried, and then Barney—Barney, the jewel, who was now in America.

"The finest little fella ye'd see between this an' County Cork! Over six fut, he is, an' wid a pair o' shoulders on him that ye'd think 'ud hardly get in through that door beyant."

"Lonneys!" said Kate admiringly.

"Aye, indeed, an' ye ought to see the beautiful black curly head of him, an' eyes like sloes, an' cheeks—why I declare"—half raising herself and speaking with great animation, "he's the very moral o' St. Patrick over there! God forgive me for sayin' such a thing, but raly if I was to drop down dead this minute I couldn't but think it! Now, I assure ye, Miss Mahony, he's the very image of that blessed statye, 'pon me word!"

Miss Mahony looked appreciatively at the representation of the patron of Ireland, which was remarkable no less for vigor of outline and coloring than for conveying an impression of exceeding cheerfulness, as both the saint himself and the serpent which was wriggling from beneath his feet were smiling in the most affable manner conceivable.

"Mustn't he be the fine boy!" she ejaculated, after a pause. "I'd love to see him—but I'll niver get a chanst o' that, I s'pose. Will he be comin' here to see ye, ma'am?"

"He'll be comin' to take me out of it," returned the mother. "He doesn't raly know I'm in it at all. I'll tell ye now the way it is. When the poor father died—the light o' heaven to him—an' bad times come, and we had to give up our own beautiful little place, Barney brought me to town an' put me with Mrs. Byrne, a very nice respectable woman that was married to a second cousin o' my poor husband's, an' I was to stop with her till he came back from America with his fortune made. Well," pursued Mrs. Brady, drawing in her breath with a sucking sound, which denoted that she had come to an interesting part of her narrative, " well, he kep' sendin' me money, ye know, a pound or maybe thirty shillin' at a time—whenever he could, the poor boy, an' I was able to work the sewin'-machine a little, an' so we made out between us till I took this terrible bad turn. Well, of course troubles niver comes single, an' the last letther I got from my poor little fella had only fifteen shillin' in it, an' he towld me he had the bad luck altogether, but says he, ' My dear mother, ye must on'y howld out the best way ye can. There's no work to be got in this place at all (New York I think it was). But I am goin' out West,' says he, ' to a place where I'm towld there's fortunes made in no time, so I'll be over wid ye soon,' he says, ' wid a power o' money an' I'm sure Mary Byrne 'll be a good friend to ye till then. The worse of it is,' he says, ' it's a terrible wild outlandish place, and I can't be promisin' ye many letthers, for God knows if there'll be a post-office in it at all,' says he, ' but I'll be thinkin' of ye often, an' ye must keep up your heart,' he says. Well," sucking up her breath again, " poor Mrs. Byrne done all she could for me, but of course when it got to be weeks an' months that I was on my back not able to do a hand's turn for meself. an' no money comin' an' no sign o' Barney, what could she do, poor cratur ? One day

Dr. Isaacs says to her, 'Mrs. Byrne,' says he, 'why don't ye send poor Mrs. Brady to the Infirmary?' 'What Infirmary, sir?' says she. 'The Union Infirmary,' says he, 'it's the on'y place she's fit for except the Incurables in Dublin,' says he, 'an' I'm afraid there's no chance for her there. 'Oh, docther, don't mention it!' says poor Mrs. Byrne—she was telling me about it aftherwards. 'Is it the Union? I wouldn't name it,' she says, 'to a decent respectable woman like Mrs. Brady. She's a cousin by marriage o' me own,' she says, 'I wouldn't *name* it to her, I assure ye.' 'Just as you please,' says Docther Isaacs. 'It 'ud be the truest kindness you could do her all the same, for she'd get betther care and nourishment than you could give her.' Well, poor Mrs. Byrne kep' turnin' it over in her mind, but she raly couldn't bring herself to mention it nor wouldn't, on'y she was druv to it at the end, the crature, with me bein' ill so long, an' the rent comin' so heavy on her an' all. So we settled it between the two of us wan day, an' she passed me her word to bring me Barney's letther—if e'er a wan comes—the very minute she gets it, an' if he comes himself she says she won't let on where I am, all at wanst, but she'll tell him gradual. Sometimes I do be very unaisy in me mind, Miss Mahony, I assure ye, wondherin' what he'll say when he hears. I'm afeared he'll be ready to kill me for bringin' such a disgrace on him."

"Sure, what could ye do?" said Kate, a little

tartly, for naturally enough, as "an inmate" of many years' standing, she did not quite like her new friend's insistence on this point. "Troth, it's aisy talkin', but it's not so aisy to starve. An' afther all, there's many a one that's worse off nor us here, I can tell ye, especially since the Sisthers come, God bless them, with their holy ways. How'd ye like to be beyant at the —— Union, where the nurses gobbles up all the nourishment that's ordhered for the poor misfortunate cratures that's in it, an' leaves thim sthretched from mornin' till night without doin' a hand's turn for them. Aye, an' 'ud go near to kill them if they dar'd let on to the Docther. Sure, don't I know well how it was before the Sisthers was here—we have different times now, I can tell ye. Why, that very statye o' St. Pathrick that ye were talkin' of a while ago, wasn't it them brought it? An' there's St. Joseph over in the ward fornenst this, an' St. Elizabeth an' the Holy Mother above. See that now. Isn't it a comfort to be lookin' at them holy things, and to see the blessed Sisthers come walkin' in in the mornin' wid a heavenly smile for every one, an' their holy eyes lookin' into every hole an' corner an' spyin' out what's wrong?"

"Aye, indeed," assented Mrs. Brady, a little faintly, though, for however grateful she might be, and comfortable in the main, there was a bitterness in the thought of her "come down" that nothing could alleviate.

She and her neighbor were excellent friends all the same, and she soon shared Kate's enthusiasm for "the Sisthers," finding comfort moreover in the discovery that Sister Louise understood and sympathized with her feelings, and was willing to receive endless confidences on the subject of the "little boy," and to discuss the probability of his speedy advent with almost as much eagerness as herself.

But all too soon it became evident that unless Barney made great haste another than he would take Mrs. Brady "out of" the workhouse. Grim death was approaching with rapid strides, and one day the priest found her so weak that he told her he would come on the morrow to hear her confession and to give her the last Sacraments.

Not one word did the old woman utter in reply. She lay there with her eyes closed and her poor old face puckered up, unheeding all Kate Mahony's attempts at consolation. These, though well meant, were slightly inconsistent, as she now assured her friend that indeed it was well for her, and asked who wouldn't be glad to be out o' that; and in the next moment informed her that maybe when she was anointed she might find herself cured an' out, as many a wan had before her, an' wasn't it well known that them that the priest laid his holy hands on, as likely as not took a good turn immaydiate.

Later on Sister Louise bent over Mrs. Brady with gentle reassuring words.

"God knows best, you know," she said, at the end of her little homily, "you will say, 'His will be done,' won't you?"

"Sure, Sisther, how can I?" whispered Mrs. Brady, opening her troubled eyes, her face almost awful to look on in its gray pallor. "How can I say, 'His will be done,' if I'm to die in the workhouse? An' me poor little boy comin' as fast as he can across the say to take me out of it, an' me breakin' my heart prayin' that I might live to see the day! An' when he comes back he'll find the parish has me buried. Ah, Sisther, how am I to resign meself at all? In the name o' God how *am* I to resign meself?"

The tears began to trickle down her face, and Sister Louise cried a little too for sympathy, and stroked Mrs. Brady's hand, and coaxed and cajoled and soothed and preached to the very best of her ability; and at the end left her patient quiet but apparently unconvinced.

It was with some trepidation that she approached her on the morrow. Mrs. Brady's attitude was so unusual that she felt anxious and alarmed. As a rule the Irish poor die calmly and peacefully, happy in their faith and resignation; but this poor woman stood on the brink of eternity with a heart full of bitterness, and a rebellious will.

Mrs. Brady's first words, however, reassured her.

"Sisther, I'm willin' now to say, 'His will be done.'"

"Thank God for that," cried Sister Louise fervently.

"Aye. Well, wait till I tell ye. In the night, when I was lying awake, I took to lookin' at St. Pathrick beyant, wid the little lamp flickerin' an' flickerin' an' shinin' on his face, an' I thought o' Barney, an' that I'd niver see him agin, an' I burst out cryin'. 'Oh, St. Pathrick!' says I, 'how'll I ever be able to make up my mind to it at all?' An' St. Pathrick looked back at me rale wicked. An' 'oh,' says I, again, 'God forgive me, but sure how can I help it?' An' there was St. Pathrick still wid the cross look on him p'intin' to the shamrock in his hand, as much as to say 'there is but the wan God in three divine Persons, an' Him ye must obey.' So then I took to baitin' me breast an' sayin', 'the will o' God be done!' an' if ye'll believe me, Sisther, the next time I took heart to look at St. Pathrick there he was smilin' for all the world the moral o' poor Barney. So, says I, 'afther that!' Well, Sisther, the will o' God be done! He knows best, Sisther alanna, doesn't He? But," with a weak sob, "my poor little boy's heart 'ill be broke out an' out when he finds I'm afther dyin' in the workhouse!"

"We must pray for him," said the Sister softly; "you must pray for him and offer up the sacrifice that God asks of you, for him. Try not to fret so much. Barney would not like you to fret. He would grieve terribly if he saw you like this."

"Heth, he would," said Mrs. Brady, sobbing again.

"Of course he would. But if he heard you were brave and cheerful over it all, it would not be half so bad for him."

Mrs. Brady lay very quiet after this, and seemed to reflect.

When the priest came presently to administer the Sacraments of the dying to her, she roused herself and received them with much devotion; and presently beckoned Sister Louise to approach.

"Sisther, when Barney comes axin' for me, will ye give him me bades an' the little medal that's round me neck, an' tell him I left him me blessin'—will ye, dear?"

"Indeed I will."

"God bless ye. An' tell him," speaking with animation and in rather louder tones. "Tell him I didn't fret at all, an' died quite contint an' happy an'—an' thankful to be in this blessed place where I got every comfort. Will ye tell him that, Sisther alanna?"

The Sister bowed her head: this time she could not speak.

* * * * *

It was nearly two months afterwards that Sister Louise was summoned to the parlor to see "Mr.

Brady " who had recently arrived from America, and to whom his cousin, Mrs. Byrne, had broken the news of his mother's death.

Sister Louise smiled and sighed as she looked at this big, strapping, prosperous-looking young fellow, and remembered his mother's description of him. The black eyes and curly hair and rosy cheeks were all there, certainly, but otherwise the likeness to " St. Patrick " was not so very marked.

" Mr. Brady wants to hear all about his poor mother, Sister," said the Sister Superior. " This is Sister Louise, Mr. Brady, who attended your poor mother to the last."

Mr. Brady, who seemed a taciturn youth, rolled his black eyes towards the newcomer and waited for her to proceed.

Very simply did Sister Louise tell her little story, dwelling on such of his mother's sayings, during her last illness, as she thought might interest and comfort him.

" There are her beads, and the little medal, which she always wore. She left them to you with her blessing."

Barney thrust out one large brown hand and took the little packet, swallowing down what appeared to be a very large lump in his throat.

" She told me," pursued the Sister in rather tremulous tones, " to tell you that she did not fret at all at the last, and died content and happy. She did, indeed, and she told me to say that she was thankful to be here——"

But Barney interrupted her with a sudden incredulous gesture, and a big sob. "Ah, whisht, Sisther!" he said.

THEO. GIFT.

DOROTHY BOULGER (Theo. Gift) is the second daughter of the late Thomas Havers, Esq., of Thelton Hall, Norfolk. and is descended from a long race of Catholic ancestors. In 1854 Theo. Gift's father became manager of the Falkland Islands, in which remote and desolate colony she and her brothers and sisters passed seven years of their childhood.

In 1861 the family left the Falkland Islands for Monte Video, the capital of Uruguay, where they remained until the death of Mr. Havers, in 1870, which brought his children back to England. It was then that his second daughter began her literary life in earnest. "Theo. Gift's" first published stories appeared in *The Galaxy*, New York, and she became almost immediately a regular contributor to that magazine. Very soon, however, after her arrival in England she managed to obtain a name and a footing for herself in the English magazines. Her first three-volume novel, "True to Her Trust," was published anonymously, but was quickly followed by "Pretty Miss Bellew," which ran, first of all, as a serial in *Cassell's Magazine*, and was the book which made her name. It was followed by "More than a Woman's Love," a serial story, which appeared in *The Lamp* under the editorship of the Rev. William Lockhart, and "Maid Ellice." These were succeeded by "Visited on the Children," "A Matter of Fact Girl," "Lil Lorimer," "A Garden of Girls," "Victims," and "Dishonored," among three-volume novels, and "An Innocent Maiden," and "Not for the Night Time," one volume each, and "The Little Colonists" and "Cape Town Dickey," books for children; besides an enormous number of short stories, sketches, essays and poems.

In 1879 "Theo. Gift" married Professor Boulger, the well-known botanist and geologist, and author of many scientific works. Her marriage was followed shortly afterwards by a very severe illness, which laid the seeds of her almost continuous ill-health, and compelled her to cease writing altogether for a time and to take entire rest from all literary labors. Since then, indeed, she has only published three books—"An Island Princess," "Wrecked at the Outset," and "Fairy Tales from the Far East," besides contributing occasional short stories to various magazines and journals of the day.

A Soldier's Wife.

BY THEO. GIFT.

CHAPTER I.

IRISH MARY.

A SCORCHING summer's day in India. Not a day like those we get in the "merry month of May" in England, but a day when the thermometer is 95 degrees in the shade; when the sun beats down with a hot, white flame out of a white-hot sky; when the atmosphere is like the breath of an oven, scorching up the leaves on the trees and the very blood in your veins. Not a breath of wind, not a blade of grass, not a green leaf, only the dusky palm-trees standing up like shafts of heated iron against the glaring sky; only the glaring white of the road winding away into the far interior, the more glaring whiteness of the dome of an isolated mosque set in a tuft of trees, and the low, red brick walls of the "station" glowing like fire in the sunbeams!

It was in the early days of the Mutiny, those awful days of reckoning which wrote their judgment in letters of blood on a nation too proud to be prudent, and too wealthy to be wise. Already the revolt had begun. The Sepoy regiments at Meerut had risen simultaneously on a quiet Sunday afternoon and butchered officers, women, and children in one indiscriminate slaughter. At Barrackpore and Umballa, and a score of other places in the presidency, native detachments, and, in some cases, whole regiments, had mutinied, here and there massacring their white comrades and officers, and marching off in triumph, here and there overcome by the superior force of the English. Delhi itself, the mighty capital of the East, was invested. A few days more, and it was to fall with a stupendous crash, a stream of blood and ruin which was to overwhelm the army of India with an agony of horror beyond all vengeance.

And yet the Indian Government looked on calmly, unbelieving that these numerous outrages and risings were anything but isolated acts of insubordination; and while in one town English officers were being blown from the guns, and English women crucified in horrible imitation of their Lord against the city walls, their countrymen and countrywomen in another, not many leagues distant, were leading the usual pleasant, languid Indian life, ignorant of what was happening, or utterly incredulous that the like fate might at any hour descend upon themselves.

Even at little Futterhabad, a small government

depot occupied by two companies of the Sixth, and a battalion of native foot, under Captains Donaldson and Clare, they were all unconscious of any danger awaiting themselves till, two days before, a messenger from the officer in command at the neighboring town of Susi informed Captain Donaldson that some of the Sepoys there had raised cries of disaffection and refused to obey orders, that the English garrison was as yet strong enough to keep them under, but that a large body of mutineers were reported as marching on the place, and the officers of the Sixth were implored to start with all speed, and so intercept these latter, as, were they once to coalesce with the disaffected within the walls, the lives of the English one and all would in all probability be the sacrifice. No time was lost in complying with the appeal contained in this dispatch; and the senior captain (Donaldson) thought himself showing extraordinary prudence in deciding not to take the native battalion with them.

"Not but that I believe our fellows to be as true as steel, but it'll be acting on the safe side not to excite them by leading them against their old comrades," he said, and Captain Clare agreeing, the regiment marched out of Futterhabad an hour before sundown, leaving behind it, besides the soldiers' wives and children and the civilians, an English sergeant and ten men to overawe (?) the native troops; as also the young wife of Captain

Clare, who had become a mother only a fortnight back.

She was not within the cantonment. The overpowering heat of the town had affected her so unfavorably in her state of health that her husband had removed her to a deserted mosque about a quarter of a mile distant from the depot, which, standing in a garden thickly overgrown with palm and tulip trees, made a pleasant sort of improvised bungalow for the invalid.

The change had agreed with her wonderfully; and when Captain Clare suggested that she should be moved back to the cantonment during his absence, she refused, declaring she would remain where she was.

"You expect to be back in thirty-six hours," she said. "What good is there in my making myself uncomfortable for so short a time?"

And Captain Clare left her, believing that there was no reason for his doing otherwise.

The fierce day had faded into evening at last, the evening of the day after his departure, and Mrs. Clare lay on her couch, her ayah squatted on the floor beside her, with the infant in her arms, and the punkah waving with monotonous regularity over her head. The croaking of the frogs could be heard distinctly from the pool in the deserted garden below, mingling with the sharp "cheep, cheep" of the lizards, and an occasional murmur from the cantonment; but it was not to those sounds that

Mrs. Clare was listening as she leaned forward on her elbow and looked out through the narrow, arched window, from which, for more air, the matted curtain had been drawn aside.

"What can it be?" she said at last. "Don't you hear it, Zeena?"

"Hear what, mem-sahib?" and the ayah ceased her rocking and crooning over the babe to look up.

"Just now there was such a strange noise from the cantonment. Can it be the Sixth returning?"

"The mem-sahib is feverish. Zeena hear nossing at all; and de Sahib Clare and de Sixth not go to come back till to-morrow."

"But we were to have heard from them to-day and there has been no message. Can anything have happened, or—there, Zeena, you must hear *that*."

"That" was audible enough indeed, a cry from the cantonment, something between a shriek and a shout, and followed by a confused hum of many voices.

"Soldier got 'bhang'—drunk—mad," said Zeena lazily. "Sergeant put him in black-hole."

"It is news of some sort from the regiment. Ah, how cruel of them not to send to me! Zeena, give me the baby and run up to the cantonment and see what it is. Make haste!" And as the lady clapped her hands impatiently, Zeena rose, and only waiting to lay the infant by its mother, sped swiftly through the low, arched doorway and disappeared into the night.

Left alone Mrs. Clare's anxiety increased. The strange rolling sound was now plainly distinguishable for the measured tramp of soldiers; and that some great excitement was going on at the cantonment was more and more evident. Once a shrill cry rose faintly into the air. Then came the sharp clang of a bell as suddenly suppressed, and yet no thought of danger there or to herself crossed her mind. Her fears were entirely with the Sixth and the husband who had marched away at their head. Could it be that they were coming back defeated, and—without him? Had no one courage to break the news to her? Twice she called aloud to the other servants, but there was no answer. Even the punkah has ceased to wave for the last few minutes.

A step roused her. A quick, noisy step coming nearer every moment. Was it her husband? No, that was no military tread; but a woman's, and one flying up the garden-walk with frantic, almost clumsy haste; another moment and the heavy curtain draping the doorway was torn aside, and a figure panting with excitement stood in the entrance.

A young woman with a sunburnt, freckled face hung round with tangled, reddish elf-locks, her bare arms hugging something like a dingy bundle of rags to her bosom, herself clad in rags of divers hues badly covered by an old plaid cloak,—such was the intruder who thrust herself into Mrs. Clare's presence: a girl, nicknamed " Irish Mary," wife to a soldier in the Sixth, but not " on the strength."

She seemed beside herself now, for after that one pause for breath she darted to the couch where the pretty patrician lady lay in her white draperies, and exclaimed in tones hoarse with excitement: " Mrs. Clare, dear, is it lyin' here ye are, as if nothin' were doin' ! Get up and fly for the love of heaven."

" Fly ! Where ? From what ? " cried Mrs. Clare, her indignation at the intrusion lost in astonishment as the other, having deposited her bundle on the bed, almost lifted her on to her feet.

" From murther an' slaughterin', an' *worse* a million times to the like o' you an' me ! " Mary cried, her rough hands busy in thrusting Mrs. Clare's little bare feet into a pair of shoes, and flinging a dark cloak which happened to come handy over her muslin wrapper. " Shure an' aren't the Sepoy divils afther enterin' the depot, an' our soldiers drugged aforehant, an' no shot fired to stay them ! Och ! bad cess to the thraitorous scoundhrels that let 'em in ! Hark to thim, dear ! There's a cry ! Och ! hurry, hurry, as ye're a livin' woman. There'll not be wan alive an hour hence ; nor we aither if we're not gone from here."

There was a desperate earnestness in the girl's eyes, but Mrs. Clare tried to resist.

"The Sepoys here!" she stammered. "Do you mean our battalion has risen?"

"An' have let in a couple of hundhred more at laste. Shure, an' wasn't I afther hearin' the thread of them as they cum up the road! Misthress, dear, for God's sake don't stan' there. There was wan of ours as wasn't drugged, Sergeant McCann he was, an' the thing I stumbled over at the gate was the dead body of him hacked thro' an' thro'. Shure an' I niver stayed till I got here; for I knew 'twas in yer bed ye were, an' none to purtect ye."

"Thank you," said Mrs. Clare faintly, and very pale, "but go yourself; Captain Clare will be back in a few hours now if he be alive, and if not, I—I would rather die here."

"*Die* is it?" cried Mary contemptuously, "an' d' ye think it's I would be afther fearin' death if that was all? Or d' ye think it's betther for the captain to fin' you a slave to the black haythens, an' yer child's brains dashed out on the stones, as they did wid the childher at Meerut? Missis dear, *I'm* flyin' for Jim's sake an' me boy's here, an' I'm not goin' widout you; for the captain's been good an' kind to Jim, an' thrated meself like the dacent wedded wife as I am (even if I'm not on the sthringth). Come, ma'am, hurry! Ye'll walk betther by yersel' than if ye were tied to a gun an' dhriven. Here, take hould of that shawl while I rowl the childher together. I'll carry them, an' you kape close to me. This way—so!"

And Mrs. Clare made no more resistance, but followed with the meekness of a child in her footsteps.

What a sight met her as they crept from out of that vaulted temple into the night air! The eastern sky was red as blood from the blazing roof of her own house in the officers' quarters; and in that scarlet light she could see the hillside and the walls of the cantonment dotted over with black figures, while the whole air seemed alive and quivering with a turmoil of shrieks, cries, and yells of agony or triumph.

One look was sufficient; and then Gertrude Clare cowered closer to the side of the Irish girl, and clung to her, murmuring: "We shall never escape! What hope is there?"

"Foller me, or it'll be thrue for ye," Mary muttered in curt response, as she dived into a dense thicket of prickly-pear and jungle-grass, trampling a path in front with her strong feet, and leaving many a fragment of her ragged garments on the thorny boughs, yet never suffering a touch to disturb the sturdy, brown-skinned eight-months' baby, or the tiny infant of scarce twice as many days, which she carried so tenderly in her right arm.

By and by Mrs. Clare stopped. They had not gone a couple of hundred yards, but she, poor girl, was faint and exhausted by the rough walking. Yet "Mary," she said, "they will be on the return march, and see the blaze. It will bring them up all the quicker, and if he finds me gone—oh! God, I know my husband—he will fling away his life in the effort to tear me from among his enemies, and I—I shall not be there."

"Wid God's blessin' ye won't indade!" said Mary solemnly, "an' niver throuble yersel'. They're not returnin' as yet, at all, at all. I heerd them black naygurs talkin' ov't as I crouched down in the scrub yonder; an' the half of them had parted off to meet the Sixth an' delay thim outside Susi till the lave o' thim had got all they wanted here."

"Where are we going then, Mary? If they are bent on destroying Captain Clare and the Sixth, where is the use of our saving ourselves?"

"Desthroy the Sixth, is it? A pack o' dhurty rebels!" cried Mary scornfully. "Shure, an' they've more thrust in the masther an' his men than yersel'. It's not hopin' to stay thim more than an hour or two they are, but "—and Mary's brown face paled and Gertrude Clare shuddered, as she added—"Misthress dear, I heerd wan say, 'Work yer wull for to-night, but take none wid ye whin ye go, not a livin' soul, man nor woman,' an' I blessed Our Lord that I'd larnt enough o' their lingo to understan'. Ask the great God to kape ye out ov their han's, and come on now. We've no time to lose."

She hurried on as she spoke, and Gertrude followed feebly, trembling in every limb, but striving with uncomplaining resolution to keep in her companion's footsteps. Did not the shrieks of those then weltering in their blood within the walls of Futterhabad cry to them to haste for life or death; for more than life, from worse than death, away! at all speed, away!

On and on, tearing their feet and hands, stooping their heads low, praying inwardly the whole time, they struggled for half an hour, the Irish girl walking with the firm, elastic tread of one well used to the march, the English one staggering after with a step momentarily slacker and more uncertain, until they found themselves on the edge of a large field of Indian corn,—and then, as Mary stooped lower with her burden, that her head might not show above the tall green stalks, Mrs. Clare gasped out:

"Go on. Save yourself. I—can do no more," and fainted away at her humble friend's feet. At the same moment the latter's baby set up a piteous wail.

Half beside herself, Mary crouched down, hushing her baby to her breast with one hand, while with the other she loosened the fainting woman's dress and turned her face upwards that the night air might refresh her. She could do no more. There was not a drop of water near to moisten the lips already black and parched, but when her child had fallen asleep again, she laid both babes down by Mrs. Clare and crept on hands and knees to a little eminence where she could have a view of their surroundings.

Poor Gertrude! She was roused from her merciful stupor by something sharp and stinging, and, opening her eyes, saw Mary leaning over her with a branch of some thorny plant in her hand; but not even the seemingly cruel method of her revival recalled her so much as the look of horror on the girl's freckled face.

"Foller me—so!" the latter whispered, and crawling behind her, Gertrude came to a point where, peeping through the sheltering stack of the Indian corn, they could see the valley beneath. They were not more than half a mile, as the bee flies, from the mosque. It lay just below them, and Gertrude, following the direction of Mary's finger, felt her blood grow chill within her veins as she saw five armed figures steal through the garden to the door from which the two women had so recently escaped.

The next moment they came rushing out into the garden again, beating about in search of their victim. Mary's hand closed on her companion.

"If they find our thrack an' come sthraight afther us they'll be ten minutes gettin' here," she said huskily. "Missis dear, I only ax ye to run ten minutes more. If we can but get through this field an' down towards the river I know where we can hide, an' they'll not be follerin' fur fear o' bein' cut off by our men. Only kape up yer heart fur the love o' God, an' thry."

CHAPTER II.

FOR LIFE OR DEATH.

It was a terrible position; and the young wife and mother understood it to the full. A dull, red spot burned in each white cheek, and her beautiful eyes looked glazed and distended; yet she spoke firmly:

"I will do my best, but if I drop *leave me;* it will not be your fault, and I shall not suffer long."

Mary said nothing, but squeezed the slim, white hand in her brown and horny one, and then, only waiting to lift the mercifully sleeping children, they resumed their flight.

Not for long. Before they had reached the further extremity of the maize-field Mrs. Clare had thrice stumbled. The stooping position now necessary was even more fatiguing than their up-hill climb through the scrub, and Mary stopped of her own accord, warned by the long-drawn, gasping breath that her companion's strength had well-nigh come to an end. A new idea seized her, and taking off her cloak she succeeded in strapping the infants on to her back; then making Mrs. Clare take her arm, led her on, cheering the sinking girl every now and then with an encouraging whisper.

And the perspiration poured off either brow like scalding rain; and the pitiless white moon looked down with a searching eye on the two poor hunted women; now and then a distant cry came from behind, warning them that their pursuers had found traces of their passage. It was down-hill now; but every step was a stumble, every breath a prayer; and they had gained such a little distance!

Suddenly Mrs. Clare reeled, and the hold on Mary's arm gave way. The red spots on her cheeks had died out and a mortal pallor was there instead.

"Mary," she said, every breath coming with a moan, "leave me now—I command it. You've done your best—God bless you—go, take your child, and give me mine. It could not live long without me; and I can go no further; not one step."

And looking in her face Mary Kirwan saw it was true. For a moment she stood still and mute, then a scarlet color rushed into her cheeks, and she fell on her knees.

"O Lord Christ! I see a way, but it's hard, hard. Help me to do it; for there's no other at all."

It was a moment's prayer, and no sooner uttered than she rose, undid the children from her back, handed Mrs. Clare her own, and tenderly wrapping up the other in her cloak darted away with it among the corn-stalks without a word.

When she came back her arms were empty, and her face was white as death.

"Mary!" cried the English mother, "where is it? What have you done with it—your child?"

"I've put it down," said Mary, her lips quivering as she raised the other. "Maybe they'll not be afther seein' him (for it's in a little hole he is among the corn) widout he cries; and he'll not do that, the darlin', when I've nursed him but the now, an' wrapped him up warm to slape."

"But Mary—my God! What do you mean?"

"Mane! shure, that I can't carry you and the childher too," said Mary simply; "an' it's thrue, ye *can't* walk no further. Och! don't be talkin', but hould yer own tight while I lift ye. Shure it's not the feather-weight ye are. Don't be talkin', I say," checking with an almost fierce authority the resistance which Mrs. Clare would fain have offered as she was lifted from the ground. "But iv ye never yet axed the Mother o' God to pray for you an' yours, ax her now, as you're a mother yersel', for me."

And on she strode as she spoke, walking far more swiftly now under her burden than when she had to accommodate her steps to the fragile creature behind her; though now and then a sob broke from her bosom, rending the heart of the prostrate girl she carried.

Yet it was not the weight which distressed her. This delicate, slender-limbed young thing, with her baby in her arms, weighed less in reality than the keg of spirits or water with which Mary had often marched behind the Sixth, or the creel of turf under which she used to tramp her native hills. It was the mother's heart in her, fighting and breaking for that sturdy, brown-skinned infant whom every step put farther and farther from her, and still she hurried on more swiftly for the agony in her mind, sometimes running, sometimes stumbling, sometimes nearly falling; never daring to pause, or lift her head once for a single breath. And still the cries of the massacre, broken every now and then by a shot fired after some stray fugitive followed them; and still the red flames of the burning cantonment filled the sky with a wild, red glow, still their pursuers kept upon their track.

A race for life or death, for honor or slavery, burdened with the increased weight of a fainting woman, flying along under the black shadow of the prickly-pear hedges, crouching among the jungle-grass in the open space till the moon, passing behind a cloud, enabled the Irish girl to pursue her perilous journey; scrambling through fields of cotton, losing her way more than once in a "tope," or grove, of feathery tamarinds, and tulip-trees, matted and woven together with creepers, whose dazzling hues by day would have made rich the conservatory of an emperor, still on, on with one prayer in her heart that the waning night might be delayed yet a little longer till she had reached a shelter she knew of, namely, an ancient tomb half hidden among jungle and creepers in a thicket near the river.

And she did. As the eastern sky flushed into a delicate rose-color, tinting earth and cloud with an ineffable, opaline glory, her sore and wearied feet stumbled heavily into the thicket of which she had been in search. As the mighty globe of day rose above the horizon, flooding all India in one second with its dazzling light, the Irish girl passed under the ruined arch of the tomb, and dropped upon the dank earth within with a cry of thankfulness half inaudible from fatigue.

They were safe.

And Mrs. Clare, rising to her knees, took the brown hands to which she owed her life in her little fingers, covering them with tears and kisses as again and again she poured thanks and blessings on her preserver. Mary checked her.

"Whisht! Not a word above yer breath! Shure, an' I'm hearin' somethin' passin' the now."

Men's voices were indeed audible, laughing and talking loudly along the road, but whether they were deserters, or only coolies on their way to labor, the women could not tell, as they cowered in the inmost recesses of their sanctuary, not even venturing for the next half-hour to creep out to drink at a little muddy pool among the reeds, which grew thickly all round them, though their lips and throats were so parched and swollen by this time, that they had hardly been able even to whisper a word to one another.

Mrs. Clare, with great discretion, drank sparingly; and would fain have coaxed Mary to do the same; but the latter plunged her hot face deep into the water, swallowing it in gulps, and only replying when she had slaked her thirst to the full.

"Lave me alone. It's got to last me till I get back."

"Back! where?" Mrs. Clare asked, but was abashed by the reply.

"Shure, an' is it lave me child fur good I'd be doin'?"

Gertrude burst into tears. Her long fainting-fit had confused her, and she now reproached herself bitterly.

"Ah, how could I let you! And you whom I've often looked down on! Why didn't you leave me instead?"

"You're a woman yersel'," said Mary gently. "An' could *you* be afther lavin' a feller-woman now to the marcy o' thim black divils? As to the boy, acushla"—her plain features working unrestrainedly with the sorrow she tried not to express in words—"wasn't it betther to lave him awhile, an' he slapin' like an angel in me ould cloak, that's for all the world the color o' the groun'? Shure, I tuk him to the font meself afore iver we left Calcutta, as is more than iver ye've been afther doin' for yours I'll be boun', the purty, wee craythur! so I'd the clane right to say to our blessed Lord, 'It's *You* he belongs to now, so take care ov him till I'm comin' back, for it's meself is takin' care of a poor unbelavin' sowl for You,' I said."

"But, Mary," cried Mrs. Clare, weeping more freely for the girl's simplicity and confidence, "don't go *now*. It will be only throwing away your own life, and if they have discovered him—oh! please God they have not!—it will be too late to save him. Don't, Mary! The Sixth will be here in a few hours hence, and then we will go back together and search for him, and he shall never want for anything again if I can help it, or you either. Only stay!"

But Mary shook her rough head doggedly.

"I could thrust Him above to help me when I was thryin' to help Him," she said, "but ef 'twas carin' for meself I was—an' shure anyhow is it I could sit here, an' me purty, bright-eyed boy, Jim's one bairn, tugging at me heart-sthrings the while?"

And yet it was with a stern, beautiful patience that she delayed another ten minutes to feed Mrs. Clare's tiny infant which had wakened crying with a hunger which its poor young mother had no power to relieve. Then, her work of charity completed, the private's wife gave the babe back to its mother, and sallied forth on the return search for her child.

Left alone the hours passed wearily with the officer's wife. She was worn out with fatigue and agitation. She was faint with hunger, and, do what she would, her child wailed and fretted as if in pain, keeping her in constant alarm lest the noise should lead to their discovery.

The sun rose higher and higher, till the low entrance to the ruin glowed like the yellow mouth of a furnace. The child, tired with crying, fell asleep again; and she herself was resting in a sort of half-slumber of exhaustion, when a noise from without startled her to a sitting position, her heart sick with terror. There was a clatter of horses' feet, and the regular tramp of many men coming up the road.

Was it the Sixth? Or was it the party of the mutineers which had separated from their fellows?

If it were the former, they might pass on, never suspecting her presence, and leave her to perish of hunger and weakness. If the latter, and she were to show herself, God only could foresee her fate in its full horror. And the tramp, tramp came nearer and nearer. She could catch, now and then, the gleam of arms among the trees which hid the ruin.

The suspense became intolerable. Laying her child gently in a dark corner, she crawled to the entrance and looked out. A body of troops were passing. She could see the scarlet uniforms of the Sixth, and the Scotch caps and gray jackets of

Captain Donaldson's men as, at quick march and in double file, they passed along, and yet when she tried to call to them her tongue clove to her mouth, a mist rose before her eyes, and with a faint cry she sank face foremost on the ground.

When she recovered she was in her husband's arms, and his grateful tears were on her face. Little indeed did that young officer, who, on the return march, had heard of the attack on Futterhabad and the wholesale massacre of every man, woman, and child of white blood, expect to see his wife alive and safe. The Sixth had met and defeated the party of which they were in search with more ease than they had expected, and were in consequence returning rather earlier, when they met *en route* the body of mutineers despatched for that purpose, who, by first harassing and then leading them in pursuit, had without the loss of more than two or three men contrived to delay them two good hours on their way.

* * * * *

And Mary?

Neither you, nor I, nor any one save those English women who passed through the agonies of that Indian " reign of terror " can tell what this girl endured in her return search for her child.

It was then in the last week of May, and the heat at eight o'clock was so intense that it seemed to frizzle the brains in her uncovered head. She had lost a shoe, and her feet were cut and swollen. Her head felt swollen too, and her eyes were dim and distended; as the sun grew hotter and hotter a species of delirium seemed to seize her. She saw before her a crowd of Sepoys with inflamed eyes and dark ferocious faces, and in the midst of them her baby held on high by one of the miscreants in the act to dash its brains out upon the ground. She shrieked aloud in her agony, darted wildly forward, stumbled, fell headlong to the ground, staggered to her feet again; and lo! the Sepoys were gone, and instead her child was wailing, wailing somewhere in front of her. Yes, she saw it now distinctly, wrapped in the cloak as she had left it among the corn-stalks, and near it, crouching for a spring, a huge Bengal tiger. Again she screamed and sprang forward, throwing out her arms wildly to scare the animal, and again the horrible vision vanished—only to be renewed a thousand times in a thousand different forms.

And then, all at once, the weight rolled off her brain, and the red mist from before her eyes. She was on her knees in the maize-field, and in front of her was the very hole where she had laid her infant, with the rusty plaid cloak crumpled on the edge of it.

But the child?

For the moment an awful despair seized her, and a cry broke from her lips so shrill and unearthly that it scared away a couple of vultures who were hovering low over something a yard or two distant. A little cooing, gurgling note of pleasure answered, and turning she saw a round rosy face among the corn-stalks and a pair of fat hands, and naked, dimpled feet trying, by stretching and crawling, to get at the mother who had left it.

When Captain Clare, accompanied by four of his men, entered the same field to search for his wife's preserver, they found Mary quietly seated on the ground nursing her baby, and the ringing cheer which greeted the sight might have shown her how her heroism was appreciated by those brave, rugged hearts. She hardly heeded it; but just stood up, dropping her courtesy to the officer, and then looked round at the others.

" An' where's my Jim at all ? "

There was no answer. The men did not seem to hear, and Captain Clare began urging her, in an agitated way, to hasten with him to the carriage at the foot of the hill where Mrs. Clare was waiting for her. Mary courtesied again.

" Thank ye, sur. 'Tis very good ye are to me: but I'm not wantin' to lave me husband, though it's not ' on the stringth ' I am. Shure, I'll go down to him the now, since he's no mind to come up to me. Maybe, though, he's not got lave to fall out o' the ranks for that."

The last words were said piteously, her eager blue eyes lifted to the officer's kindly face. Very gently he took her arm.

"Come to the carriage first, Mary, anyway. Mrs. Clare wants to—to speak to you. My good girl, my brave girl, you're not going to give way now?"

"Is it *kilt* he is?" she asked hoarsely; and then before any reply could be given save the mute answer of the eyes, the child fell from her arms, she reeled suddenly, and dropped a senseless, crumpled heap at the commander's feet.

BARONESS PAULINE VON HÜGEL.

PAULINE MARIE VON HÜGEL was born at Florence, where her father was Austrian envoy to the Duke of Tuscany When still in her teens, having lost her father, she went to reside in England with her mother, by birth a Scotchwoman. She first began to write for *The Catholic Fireside*, in which appeared short lives of St. Cecilia, St. Benedict, St. Francis, and St. Ignatius, as well as several tales. She has written the " Price of the Pearl," published by the Catholic Truth Society, a sketch of Lady Clare Feilding for *The Catholic Magazine*, and " Carmen's Secret," which, after coming out in *The Catholic Magazine*, is to be republished in book-form by the Catholic Truth Society.

Fair Dorothy Wilmot.

BY BARONESS PAULINE VON HÜGEL.

CHAPTER I.

"Joan, Joan, what think you? Her Grace and my Lord Cardinal are dead!"

The speaker was my dear lady, the beautiful Mistress Dorothy Wilmot, and the event of which she did apprise me was the death of the Queen of England and her kinsman, Cardinal Pole.

"God rest their souls!" I cried, suffering the work I held to drop into my lap; "'tis evil days we have to look for now!"

"Nay, Joan," said my mistress, "give not place to doleful dumps—methinks thou art not unlike a raven in thy black gown and with thy black eyes—those black eyes of thine are wont to tinge what they see with somewhat of their own hue. What cause is there for fear? Will not the Lady Elizabeth be Queen now? Stay, thou wert not by when my father told of what took place but two weeks ago! 'Tis the King of Spain, it seems, hath favored her succession—is he not as good a Papist as thyself? And, to make the matter more secure, Her Grace sent for the Lady Elizabeth, and before she would name her heir to the throne, required a solemn promise of fidelity to the Catholic faith; and then my Lady Elizabeth did confirm the sincerity of her belief in the strongest words, and prayed God that 'the earth might open and swallow her up if she were not a true Roman Catholic.' What sayest thou now, Joan?"

"That words are cheap, Mistress Dorothy, and that perchance to the Lady Elizabeth England's crown seemeth worth a lie—nay, be not angry—all may be mighty well, but do men gather grapes of thorns, or figs of thistles? When they do, then shall a daughter of King Henry and Anne Boleyn be what we would have her be."

"And when a Queen shall be to thy entire liking, then, my good Joan, shall we be living in Utopia, the land of which that wise man, Thomas More, did write. Was not Queen Mary too Catholic for thy liking?"

"Nay, not too Catholic," I made answer; "that could not be; but persecution misliketh me sore; did not the Lord of the harvest say that the wheat and cockle should be suffered to grow together until the end, when He, not Queen or Parliament, would see to the burning of the cockle? 'Tis not, believe me, the best Catholics that have advised the excellent Queen to these strong measures; 'tis rather some who would have Her Grace think them good

Catholics by showing this unhallowed zeal, and who, I misdoubt me sore, will be among the first to shuffle off their ill-fitting Popery when their new sovereign shall bid them do so."

My lady's blue eyes began to flash, and I dared say no more. Somewhat haughtily she bade me get together her best wearing apparel, as full soon she and her father would be travelling up to London to see the new queen pass through the town in state. "But thou canst tarry here an thou dost list," she added coldly; "I can dispense thee from thy service."

And so my lady left me to my thoughts. Why was Mistress Dorothy thus discomposed? The reason was not far to seek, but ere I tell it, let me say a few words touching other matters, and, first of all, concerning Joan, her waiting-maid. My mother had come over from Spain to the service of Queen Katharine, had married in England, and early left a widow, had sent me across the seas to be brought up in a nunnery, while she took service once more, this time with my Lady Wilmot. That lady soon learned to love the trusty waiting-woman right well, and it was through her good offices that the little wench in the foreign convent, who had displayed quick parts and a thirst for knowledge, was trained up somewhat beyond her station. But calamity was to befall poor Joan—she married young, and she too, like her mother, was early left a portionless widow, and then Joan's first thought was to return to England and take service with my Lady Wilmot, and if possible fill the vacancy left by the sudden death of her valued waiting-woman. I shall never forget my coming unto Chesney Court, and my Lady Wilmot's kindness. She was a most sweet lady, good and beautiful,—though not so beautiful as Mistress Dorothy. The dear lady looked at me long and searchingly, and then she did embrace me. " God bless thee, Joan," said she earnestly, " thou art come to be to Dorothy what thy mother was to me, the faithfullest of serving-women—but be thou yet more than this. If I mistake not, thou canst read men and women as well as books—be Dorothy's *friend* when I am gone."

I marvelled at these words, but at that moment entered my lord, and with him Mistress Dorothy.

How shall I describe my mistress as I first saw her in the fair sunset of that summer evening! The maid was scarce sixteen years of age, tall and most exceeding comely—her golden hair framed a face fairer and sweeter than any I have ever seen. Some little pride and wilfulness were, perchance, written in the curves of the delicate lips; the blue eyes looked resolute and true as well as loving, but, above all, on the fair countenance there was that look of candid innocence which, methinks, the Lord must have seen writ on the brow of the young man whom straightway, as He looked upon, He loved. My heart as well as mine eyes had seemed to travel forth to greet the comely maiden; I went up to Mistress Dorothy—my gift from God, given by Him to fill the aching empty place in my heart. "I am your serving-woman and friend, madam, all the days of my life," I said, bowing low before her. She smiled, and the whole fair face seemed lit up as though by brightest sunshine.

"Dear Joan," she said, stooping down to kiss me, "nay, what a little body thou art to be so old and wise! Thou shalt teach me much of thy foreign lore, for I too have a mind to be learned."

At this my lord burst out a-laughing. "What" quoth he, "art thou not fair enough, Doll, to find a husband whether thy head be full or empty?"

Whereat Mistress Dorothy frowned, and tapped her foot impatiently. "'Tis for my own use, sir, not a husband's," she made answer, "that I would fain furnish my head." Whereat my lord laughed the more, but my lady chid her daughter gently for being too forward with her answers.

Soon after Joan's coming my lady's health, as she doubtless had foreseen, began rapidly to decline, and she grew so feeble ere the winter had come 'twas a wonder she had spirit enough left to crave my lord to carry herself and all of us to London to witness the most memorable and touching sight I ever did behold. The Cardinal bearing the Pope's pardon to this realm had been escorted in triumph from Dover. At Gravesend he entered the royal barge to which he did affix his silver rood

—ah, me! 'twas goodly that the sign of our salvation should be publicly honored in this land again. And now, on the feast of St. Andrew, the Cardinal did solemnly absolve the nation from its apostasy. We knelt as we heard the great "Amen" ring out into the still air, and round about were strong men, as well as women, weeping and striking their breasts as they cried out, "This day are we born again!"

We received the Cardinal's blessing after the Mass as he made his way past his kneeling fellow-countrymen, from whom he had been an exile because of his fidelity to Rome. Then did we hurry to Paul's Cross to hear Chancellor Gardiner preach to the multitude, bewailing sore that he had not withstood His Majesty as he ought touching the supremacy, and calling on those who in times so perilous had flinched or faltered, to seek Christ's pardon with himself. But the crowning grace, it seemed to me, was when the Most Holy Sacrament was carried through the streets of the great city that like Jerusalem had been so faithless to its Lord—the banners gleamed, the censers waved, and from a hundred hundred hearts and lips burst forth the cry, "Lauda Sion salvatorem! What think you must those generous souls have felt who through evil report, as well as now in good report, who in prisons and stripes beyond measure had ever remained faithful and true?

That evening my lady retired to rest somewhat

early, wearied with the fatigues of the day. When I had fulfilled my little duties about her person she did take hold of my hand. "Joan," said she, a happy light shining in her eyes, "I can sing my 'nunc dimittis' now—England is Catholic and my lord is reconciled unto the Church. My dear daughter I leave unto thy care; promise me, a dying woman, never to leave her, to help her through the many perils of the world."

"I will serve her," I made answer, "all the days of my life, but, alack! a poor waiting-woman scarce a dozen years her senior, can hope for little influence over one of her quality and high spirit."

My lady sighed. "Ah, child," she said, "I am leaving this world of lying shadows for the land of truth and substance—thinkest thou my poor Dorothy's quality or fair face will avail her there? Methinks she may need a friend more than the poorest, most ill-conditioned wench in all this great city. To thee do I this day most solemnly commit her."

"I will do my best, my very best," I answered through my tears, "that beyond Jordan Mistress Dorothy and you may meet, never to part again."

Ere Christmastide had come and gone the poor of Chesney Court had lost a constant friend, my lord the best and gentlest of wives, and my dear mistress, young, beautiful, and headstrong, was left without a mother, to face the dangers of the great world.

CHAPTER II.

Four years passed by and Mistress Dorothy was a child no longer. Her father was proud beyond measure of his daughter's comeliness and parts; moreover it was to her alone that he could look to advancing the fame of his house, for other children had he none. Yet more than one goodly alliance did Mistress Dorothy reject, till the day came—ah, me, how well I mind it now!—when, casting her arms about my neck, she did cry, "What think you, Joan; I have parted with my heart at last!"

"To whom, dear soul?" quoth I. "Unto some one worthy of thy favor, I do trust, and of the right sort touching religion?"

"Yea," said she, with that smile like to sunshine, "'tis my Lord Erdleigh—is he not a good enough Papist to please even thee, mine own dear Joan?"

Her words sent a cold chill to my heart. Lord Erdleigh was a gentleman nigh twenty years her senior—handsome, rich, and in very good favor at the court, but, alack! I wholly mistrusted him. In the days of King Henry he had taken the oath of supremacy, and in return had been rewarded with a goodly share of Church property; his zeal had gone further in his late Majesty's reign—he was a stanch upholder of the new doctrines and had been, so it was rumored, the familiar friend of Cranmer. He was a zealous Papist now, none could deny that; more than once at assemblies had he dropped his beads from his doublet, and on his friends making somewhat merry thereat, had replied gravely, "I always carry the like about with me to insure the protection of Heaven." Moreover, he was one of those who most advised the Queen sternly to persecute heretics, and affected to be sore scandalized with some of the English hierarchy, and Cardinal Pole in especial, for saying: "Bishops should look on those who erred as sick children, and not for that to slay them," and that "Bishops ought not to seek the death, but rather to instruct the ignorance of their misguided brethren."

"Oh, my dear, dear lady!" was all I could say, in deep distress.

"Nay, what ails thee?" she cried impatiently. "Hath not my lord found favor with Her Majesty —be not that a pledge of loyalty to Rome?"

"A better would have been," I answered boldly, "had he been reconciled to the Church of Christ, without waiting first to be assured that he should retain his ill-gotten goods. Would there were more like Her Majesty, who hath given up many thousands of yearly revenue, saying with noble spirit to those who would have withheld her therefrom, 'I value the peace of my conscience more than ten such crowns as that of England.'"

Woe's me! In my zeal how had I lacked discretion! Mistress Dorothy was a great lover of my lord, her father—he had never gone so far as my Lord Erdleigh, either against Pope or heretics, but he had waited for reconcilement with the Church till the Cardinal had brought assurances from Rome that holders of monastic property should be left in undisturbed possession. I could plainly see by Mistress Dorothy's visage that I had displeased her sore.

" 'Tis easy work for those who have nothing to win or lose to talk mightily magnanimous," she said haughtily, " but I counsel thee, Joan, an thou wouldst tarry with me, to mind and mend thy manners, since my husband will not be one to brook churlishness or froward speeches."

" Bid me not to leave thee!" I cried passionately; " who will ever love thee as I do? Ah, mistress mine, is not thy heart great enough to pardon a few slips in courtesy in view of a life's devotion? Art thou like the rest of the world? must I fawn and flatter, and say peace, peace, when I know there is no peace? may I never for one moment forget thy quality and my nothingness, and remember only that we are both Christian women who have the same God to serve, who belong to the same great Church, who are hoping for the same glorious heaven?"

Mistress Dorothy's eyes had grown very gentle ere I had ceased speaking.

" Fear nothing, dear heart," said she; "no one in

all Christendom shall part us two—I promise it thee in my dead mother's name. But why misdoubt me so? Dost thou think I would marry my lord did I not believe him to be a true Catholic? Why am I bound to believe evil of one who hath proved himself so zealous? Methinks I am a better Christian than thou art, for I be less severe in my judgments. Hadst thou been one of the chosen twelve, sure it is thou wouldst have warned the Lord against trusting Blessed Peter any more, and declined him as thy head after his denial. Hath my lord done worse than Blessed Peter?"

I caught hold of her hand as I said: "My child, my mistress, my dear one, wilt thou give this hand of thine to a man of blood? 'Tis true the best may fall, but when they rise again they are merciful, they persecute no man, be he the worst of heretics—think of those awful burnings."

Mistress Dorothy shuddered as she cried: "Enough, enough! we women are altogether too tender; we understand not such matters. If I were Queen, 'tis certain no felon should be put to death, and then what would become of the safety of the realm? Is it not worse to kill the soul than the body. If 'tis lawful to put to death one who taketh the life of the body, is it less lawful to put to death one who goeth about destroying souls? Nay, I will not argue more, my mind is made up; I *will* marry my lord."

"When?" I asked in deep dejection.

"Nay, there be no haste in the matter," said she, smiling. "Her Grace's health is fast giving way; 'tis hardly meet for a courtier to be thinking of marriage just now."

I breathed more freely—Mistress Dorothy might still be saved! And now methinks I have brought you back to the beginning of my story.

CHAPTER III.

My dear lady's anger was but short-lived. She came to me that very same evening and said: "Thou art a troublesome woman, Joan, but for all that I love thee—thou shalt doff thy black gown and travel to London, and cry, 'Long live Queen Bess!' with the bravest of us."

"Nay," I said, laughing, "'tis not likely Her Majesty's eyes will pitch upon so small a body in so great a throng, but I am happy to be going with thee."

"Go to! thou foolish woman," the maid interrupted gayly, "who could settle my gear but thou? Thou shouldst know thine own worth better, then wouldst thou be but little moved at my naughty threats."

'Twas a goodly show, that court procession, 'twere useless to deny it. I was seated in a little coign of vantage at a casement behind Mistress Dorothy, where we could conveniently view the whole of that great pageant. But a mist overspread my eyes as a remembrance of the last pageant I had seen in the self-same city arose as a vision before me. I saw once more the censers wave and the banners gleam, the kneeling multitudes, and then the good Cardinal, loyal and true, bear-*Him* aloft, our Life, to bless us as He went by, yea, to bless us, and be blessed—" Pange lingua," " Lauda Sion salvatorem "—I heard the strains again, " Long live Queen Bess!" " Three cheers for Her Highness!" " God bless your Majesty!" These cries brought me back to the present with a start. I looked down and, lo, I did behold our new Queen! There was a slight block in the crowd, and I had leisure to note well Her Majesty's face—alack! it misliked me sore. Her bearing was full queenly, and upon her countenance 'twas easy to read a strong will, a clear judgment, a ready wit, wisdom to conceive a plan, and power to carry it out. But I saw still more clearly writ upon that sagacious visage, meanness, cruelty, treachery. My gaze seemed spellbound upon the cold blue eyes and the thin, compressed lips with their evil smile. As I thus looked my fill, the Queen glanced upward, and she for a moment seemed spellbound in her turn. 'Twas little wonder, I thought, as I turned me round. The sun was shining full upon my comely mistress; methought I had never seen her so dazzling in beauty before. Flushed and radiant, she was leaning forward crying out, " God bless the Queen!" For an instant a frown darkened that smiling royal face, as her majesty turned to one of her escort—methought to inquire the name of the beautiful maiden. The gentleman looked upward —'twas no other than my Lord Erdleigh—I could see pleasure and pride writ in his glance as he did greet his fair betrothed, but only a look of humble deference was left as, bowing low before Her Majesty, he made answer to her question.

The next moment the pageant had passed on, and my dear mistress, clapping her little hands, cried out: "What say you, Joan, does she not look every inch a Queen? But she be not over well-favored—'twould be grievous methinks to have such red hair. Of the twain 'twould please me better to have thy black locks though they be somewhat sad-looking. Didst note how nigh unto the Queen rode my Lord Erdleigh? He be good friends with Sir William Cecil, who doth stand so well with Her Highness."

"Yea," I remarked with some disdain, "'tis bruited that, seeing her late Majesty misdoubted her of his piety, Sir William Cecil said 'twas well to withdraw allegiance from the setting to the rising sun."

My Lord Erdleigh waited upon Mistress Dorothy and her father that evening. Methought my dear lady wore a somewhat troubled look after the interview, but it dispelled as, showing me a mighty fair bejewelled ring and necklet, the gifts of my lord, she said, right earnestly : "Joan, he doth in good truth honor and cherish me; I be assured of that. It seemeth Her Highness is known to be a scant favorer of the marriage of courtiers, and doth reckon a fair face as somewhat of a crime. She did ask after my name this day, and when my lord had told it, she said sharply, ' Rumor hath it, my lord, that you be about to wed that waxen Doll, or Dorothy, or whatever be her name.' But my lord saith that by good contrivance all will be well, and that for no queen in Christendom would he give me up."

"And touching matters of faith what saith my lord?" quoth I.

The troubled look came back to the sweet, candid face. "Ah, dear heart," she said, "'tis sad! The new Queen is bent upon requiring the oath of supremacy, but my Lord saith she will stop there— she will go no further than His Majesty, her father, who thou knowest full well continued Catholic unto the end."

"Not so," I said firmly. "As well would ye seek to have a ship without a helm, a house without a roof, or a man without a head, as a Catholic without the Pope."

"Joan," said my mistress sadly, "I was not made for such deep matters—I leave them to older and wiser heads than mine. I love the holy faith, but leave me the Church's blessed sacraments, Christ's dear Mother, the Mass, and all the goodly things we prize, what mattereth it to Dorothy Wilmot whether the Pope in Rome, or the Queen in London, be called head? If there be sin in the matter, the sin will lie at the door of Her Highness, not at the door of such of her loyal subjects as do but obey the Scriptures, that bid us be submissive to our rulers. Nay, Joan, trouble me not with thy disputations, which serve but to give me the headache. I must e'en let my lord think and decide for me." And thus ended a memorable and, to me, most sad day.

CHAPTER IV.

MANY months passed by at Chesney Court much after the wonted manner, save for the not infrequent comings of my Lord Erdleigh, who said if he but steered his bark aright, full confident was he of obtaining the royal sanction for his union. Thus hoped I ever against hope, that what I so greatly feared might be averted. Methought, though my lord loved my mistress, he yet loved power and advancement more. The two loves seemed hard to reconcilement, and I felt assured which of the twain would be banished from his heart, if need compelled a choice. Mayhap I misjudged him herein, not reckoning sufficiently upon the magic spell my dear mistress did ever cast over all who came nigh unto her person. Certain it is that my lord was loyal to her, and in the end obtained a somewhat ungracious consent from the Queen, through the good offices of his friend Sir William Cecil.

Lord Erdleigh's country seat was situate but some ten miles from Chesney Court, for which thing Mistress Dorothy's father was right glad, for, said he, " I shall gain me a son, and shall lose no daughter."

" God help the father of such a son," thought I, as I looked at the cold, well-favored visage of Lord Erdleigh.

Mistress Dorothy, who knew by many a little token that no love was lost between her betrothed and me, would chide me often and say, " Go to, thou foolish Joan ! Dost thou think 'tis some cuckoo come to dislodge thee from thy nest within my heart ?—but my heart be big enough for the two of ye."

" Sweet soul," I cried one day, " indeed it is not thus with me. I would be dislodged and banished from thy heart this moment could I but further thereby thy best interests, thy soul's eternal interests."

" Joan, Joan, be not afraid," she made answer, a passing shadow resting upon that sunny face. " I will be faithful to my Church as well as to my lord—fear not, 'twill all be well."

And now within a month this dreaded union was to take place. What should I do ? What could I do ? Methinks mine angel guardian must have whispered a thought of hope to me in my deep dejection. "Knowest thou not, faint heart, that St. Bernard saith, none ever implored the help of the virgin Mother of God in vain. 'No one,' saith he, not 'no saint,' 'no faithful soul,' but just plainly '*no one*,' that is no one at all. Before the feast of her Visitation this ill-omened match shall be broken off—*how* I *know* not, but our own St. Anselm saith, 'Crede tamen quod juvamen per eam recipias.'"

The time was drawing very near, my dear lady's wedding apparel was all ready, but still I hoped and prayed on. "No one, no one, O blessed Mother," I would whisper to myself, when I grew of small comfort.

At length one morning Mistress Dorothy called me to her—she held a letter in her hand.

"Joan," she said, smiling, "we will ride over this day to Erdleigh Castle with my father. My lord saith it will honor him greatly if I will choose the special chambers that please me best, that he may have them hung with the finest tapestries and adorned for my use. I warrant we find a convenient chamber for thee, too, dear Joan."

The letter she held was open and unfolded. My sight is quick and I noticed an underlined addendum on the back of the large paper. "Pardon me," quoth I, "but hast thou noted the postscript to this letter?"

"Nay," said she, hastily turning it over. She looked a little discomposed as she said: "He doth add that if this message arrive earlier than he doth reckon for, he would beg of me not to visit Erdleigh till next week, as his servitors have his armory and other chambers to set in order, which had best be done ere we visit the place—'tis no matter though, my father hath ordered out the horses. We will go this day, Joan."

"Had we not best wait?" I said faintly; anything, everything that seemed to bring the marriage less near was wondrous welcome to me. But my mistress little brooked delays once her mind was made up.

"Go on!" she cried. "Thinkest thou my lord hath a Bluebeard's closet that he would hide from view? If it matters not to me to find the place in disarray, it will matter nothing to him either—we will e'en go, the more so as the day is full pleasant."

My heart grew very heavy as we rode along. Mistress Dorothy was in high spirits, and my lord her father was bantering her most of the way. It was easy to see how much he liked the match, for all the talk turned on the good prospects of the two houses. "And what of our trusty Joan?" said my lord, in his kind, frank way; "what preferment shall she have? Methinks she looketh somewhat gloomstruck for such joyful times."

Mistress Dorothy glanced at me somewhat uneasily; the dear soul was open as the day, and knew of no concealments even in petty matters. "Joan hath a finer conscience than we be gifted with," she answered lightly; "it misliketh her that my lord hath taken the oath of supremacy to Her Highness."

My lord's visage waxed somewhat red. "Well, well," said he, "'tis not a matter for young heads and womanfolk to meddle with."

"Pardon me," I said, his constant kindness emboldening me to speak, "'tis over-bold, but I would fain know what course the Lord Wilmot meaneth to take—can he doubt which it is that the sainted lady who is now in heaven is praying that he may choose?"

I saw the tears rise to the eyes of the best of masters.

"Thou art altogether too bold for thy sex and station, Joan," he made answer, "but if thou must needs know, we in the country lag behind the frequenters of the great city. I know not yet how I shall act—time enough, time enough—what saith the Scripture, 'sufficit diei malitia sua.' Canst thou gainsay the wisdom of that?" But Mistress Dorothy, laughing somewhat uneasily, bid him remember *who* it was that could betimes quote the Holy Scriptures.

As we were not looked for, my lord bid us dismount at the castle gates, and telling the servants to take the horses to the village hostelry, we made our way to the great house. The doors were standing open—indeed, the whole building was in great confusion, waiting men and maids were running hither and thither, setting to rights the mansion that had not been much used by its owner of late years. My Lord Wilmot, like the true English gentleman that he was, straightway betook himself to the kennels and stables. My dear mistress darted hither and thither with many an exclamation of, "What think you, Joan? I had scarce credited it was so big a place! This be a fine chamber in good sooth—methinks this is the best of the withdrawing rooms." Suddenly I remembered Lord Erdleigh having once long ago praised his chapel, and the massing stuff and other rare things therein contained, and notably an ancient image of Our Lady, said to be miraculous, that the monks used to honor in the days gone by. Methought the holy spot would suit my heavy heart far better than these grand chambers. Unheeded by any one, I made my quest first at one end of the building, then at the other. At length going up a flight of steps, I did come upon what I guessed must be the entrance to the chapel. It was a vestibule in which stood a stoup for holy water. Over the doorway were painted the words "Domus Dei, porta cœli." I entered the chapel, but to my surprise found it completely empty.

As I was turning to go away after noting the beauty of the groined roof and oak panelling, a great noise in the court beneath drew me to the casement. I looked without, and what I **saw** doth haunt me still, and will, unto my dying day. Some of the servitors had apparelled themselves in the sacred vestments; one was swinging a censer, yet another was holding aloft a rood of rough workmanship to the derision of the rest. Meanwhile some half-drunken fellows, singing a song fit to make the angels weep, were lighting a bonfire into which they did cast first one holy thing and then another. They had brought forth the old time-honored image of the blessed Mother, and were about to cast it into the flames.

For a moment I stood rooted to the spot with dismay, then as I ran down into the courtyard beneath I cried aloud: "Blasphemers, cowards, traitors all of ye, how will ye answer to your master for this?"

"Heyday! what have we here?" cried one. "Dost wish, mistress, for some of this massing stuff to make thyself a Sunday's kirtle with? 'Tis not so fine neither, for my lord hath long ago carried away the best to make hangings for the chamber of my lady that is to be. Thou shouldst have seen the chalice, or cress—which be we to call it now?—'twas covered with fair jewels—they have served for a necklet and ring for my lady, it seemeth. 'Tis a shame to have left us naught but this rubbish." Their evil pranks were about to begin again, when suddenly there fell a silence upon the unhallowed crowd, as one man cried out: "Here cometh my lord," and Lord Erdleigh, in travelling-dress, betokening that he had but just arrived, walked into the midst of them.

"What be all this tomfoolery?" he said coldly, "and whom have we here?" he added, frowning, as his glance fell upon me. "Mistress Joan, ye would be better employed at Chesney Court, attending to the coifs and gowns of the fairest lady in England, than at Erdleigh Castle mixing in the revels of some drunken clowns."

"My lord," I cried, "this is not the time for me to explain, but, oh, see what these men have done! They are mocking the rood, they have impiously donned the sacred vestments, they be about to burn that image of the blessed Mother."

"What shall I do to them?" he said in mocking tones. "Perchance thou knowest not that the fires of Smithfield have gone out, but shall I cast these idle fellows into yon flames?"

"We have only obeyed my lord's orders," one man said sullenly.

"How now, sirrah?" quoth my lord angrily, "did I ever say to make all this hubbub, and to get in half the village for an orgy?"

"Your lordship said not so, but ordered all the remaining Popish stuff to be carted away out of the chapel, which was to be turned into the armory. If my lord had tarried away until the morrow, when he was expected, he would have found the work complete—no sign of the chapel left—though in good sooth there be not much trace left now, saving some Latin lines and a vat for that water which the devil abhorreth," the man added with a laugh.

"Bid the men take off these trumpery rags and cast them into the fire to be burnt with this old scarecrow of a wonder-working image," said my lord, kicking the statue contemptuously towards the flames. "I would have them cease their tomfoolery and get on with their work."

"Hold!" cried a clear ringing voice, in tones like those, methinks, with which the wondrous Maid of Orleans must have led her men to victory or death. My lord and I looked up at the same moment. At the chapel window, looking down upon the hideous scene, stood Mistress Dorothy; her face was white and there was a look of horror in the wide-opened eyes, but none of fear—that was a look no one hath ever seen on Dorothy Wilmot's face. "My lord, you will order that image of the holy Mother of God to be rescued from the flames *instantly*, or, by Heaven! I will come down and rescue it myself."

Lord Erdleigh looked at her for a moment lost in astonishment. "How came you hither?" he then cried. "Any commands of yours shall be at once obeyed." The half-charred image was brought to my lord, who asked if there were any further orders for his men. "Yea," she cried, still in that ringing voice, and with the look of horror still in the great blue eyes, "bring it to me hither—

and the rood and the massing stuff and the censer."

"Hath she gone mad?" I heard a man mutter as he carried up the things; "'tis nothing but charred rubbish. What can she want with it?"

Lord Erdleigh and I followed him to the chapel. The crowd of revellers had dispersed, and the waiting-man withdrew after bringing up his burden. "And now, my lord," quoth Mistress Dorothy, walking up to him, "will you gift me with these things?" He bowed low and waited for her to proceed. "'Tis the first gift I have ever asked, and the last I shall ever accept from thee," she continued. Her hands were clasped, and I noted that within them she held the fair bejewelled ring and necklet. "I cannot give back these to *you*," she cried, "for they were not yours to give me, you robbed them from the Holy of holies—to God must they be restored. Know that sooner would I starve, sooner would I be burnt, than have any more dealings with such an one as you."

"Ah, you will repent of this—you will indeed repent of it," said my lord, moved from his usual formal bearing by an emotion that was not anger.

"Never," she answered firmly, "never shall I repent me of throwing in my lot, at last, with what is great and true and holy—with the Church of Christ; I thank Him, oh! I thank Him that it is not yet too late."

"Fair, wilful child," he said, looking at her with

compassion and tenderness, "mayhap the days were when I, too, might have thought like you; but it is all a dream; cast not away preferment, love, honor, wealth, happiness, for a dream, a shadow."

"Thy words do not even tempt me," she made answer; "the esteem in which I held thee is dead and gone. Never again could I touch thy sacrilegious hand even in common friendship; go, my lord, go and worship 'the rising sun'—when the first smart is over thou wilt bless—not Heaven, such a man as thou has naught to do with Heaven —but the stars—thy destiny—that thou hast no Popish wife to bring a cloud between thee and the rising sun." At this moment I espied my lord her father hurrying across the court, 'twas evident he had been apprised somewhat of what had taken place. In another moment he was apprised of the rest. "And now what say you to the wilfullest as well as the fairest lady in all England?" quoth my Lord Erdleigh.

My master's visage had waxed very red and he looked sore discomfited. "Nay," he said, growing more resolute as he proceeded, "perchance— perchance—Doll hath acted right. Methought— God help me—to be wiser than the Eternal Wisdom that said, 'Ye cannot serve two masters.' The good Cardinal reconciled me to the Master I had forsaken—no, sith the royal supremacy doth bring so much of evil in its train—I—I am on the side of the Pope."

"Ye know not, ye know not," Lord Erdleigh said earnestly, "to what ye be pledging yourselves; I do happen to be apprised thereof—'twill mean fines, imprisonment, the rack, the dungeon—death itself methinks."

"The color came back to Mistress Dorothy's face, she lifted her head with noble courage—never had I seen her look fairer than as she made answer: "My lord, we have but one parting word to say—we do intend to serve Him who said, 'Fear not them that kill the body, but fear Him who can destroy both soul and body in hell.' It is He who hath promised that as the day is, so shall our strength be."

*   *   *   *   *

In a convent chapel beyond the seas there is used a fair chalice set with jewels. An image of the blessed Mother, charred and blackened as though by fire, is honored there, and the abbess, a woman of mature years, prayeth before it night and morn. An aged sister with more love than skill hath inscribed these words on a scroll beneath it: "No one hath ever had recourse to thy protection without obtaining relief." The name of the sister, it is said, used to be Joan, and the abbess was known in that world whose "fashion passeth away" as "Fair Dorothy Wilmot."

LADY AMABEL KERR.

LADY AMABEL KERR, daughter of the sixth Earl Cowper, was born in 1846. She was received into the Catholic Church in 1872, and the following year was married to Admiral Lord Walter Kerr. She is the author of a number of books, among them: "Unravelled Convictions," being the reasons for her conversion; "Before Our Lord Came," an Old Testament history for little children; "A Mixed Marriage," a novel; "Life of Joan of Arc," and "Life of Blessed Sebastian Valfre." She is at present the editor of *The Catholic Magazine*, the organ of the Catholic Truth Society, and is on the committee of the Society.

Just What was Wanted.

BY LADY AMABEL KERR.

The devastating effects of the Protestant Reformation on the religious life of the English people remind us of those of the great geological upheavals of prehistoric times. Fragments of truth, some large, some infinitesimally small, and bearing a greater or lesser resemblance to the great rock of Catholic dogma from which they have been severed, are to be found scattered about through the length and breadth of the land. Among such fragments we venture to think that the largest are to be found, not, as some might say, in the high Anglicanism of the day, in spite of its careful imitation of the Church's doctrines and ceremonies, but in those rural districts where faith and the love of God have been kept alive by dissenting revivals. Though the idea and name of the sacraments have been lost as well as their reality, a personal and realizing love of our blessed Lord has survived as the one great fact in these simple people's lives—a love which, besides the higher graces which it entails, gives a nobility, and almost a romance, to existences which without it would be to the last degree prosaic and flat. It is the story of one such as these, whose fidelity to the glimmerings of light vouchsafed to her was rewarded in God's own way, that we have to tell in these pages.

Martha Gray, a plain, middle-aged woman, poor and imperfectly educated, dwelt by herself in a little straw-thatched cottage on the outskirts of Appleton, a village in the County of ———. She had refrained from marriage, and had devoted herself with patient, unconscious heroism to the care of her old parents, bedridden and feeble in mind. It was now some years since they had both passed to another life, and Martha dwelt alone in the home of which for more than twenty years she had been the bread-winner.

There was nothing in Martha's surroundings to raise her from what was strictly commonplace. The country round, though rural, was bereft of natural beauty, and her neighbors were far from elevated. There was no great poverty in Appleton, but the rate of weekly wage was low, the labor to be performed was monotonous and deadening, the homes slatternly and unattractive, and the public-houses almost absurdly numerous. There reigned throughout the place an atmosphere of moral torpor accompanied by what must be called a brutish moral depravity, startling to those who think that innocence must prevail where the grass grows green and where the sun's rays are unimpeded.

Yet, in the midst of such surroundings, plain Martha Gray lived in a beautiful mystical world of her own, illumined by a ray of that divine love which raised St. Teresa and St. Gertrude from earth to heaven, and had made its way through the mists of heresy into this poor English peasant's soul. Her interior life was one of keenest joy, spent moment by moment in the presence of Our Lord, and in a realizing conformity of her will to His.

True to her Protestant creed Martha was her own spiritual guide, and her own judgment was her sole rule of faith. Her parents had been Methodists, but she said she did not altogether "hold with them;" nor did she attach herself to any particular body. Sometimes she attended the Wesleyan chapel, but, though she repudiated the idea of being a "churchwoman," she generally found her way to the parish church. There was something in the dignity and rhythm of the grand old prayers which appealed to her soul. She loved the hymns, and the music of the organ even as evoked by the village schoolmistress. Her nature liked the reserve, monotonous though it might be, of the Church of England service better than the emotionalism of the meeting-house. It is true that her own spiritual life was based entirely on the emotions, but she preferred to keep these for the privacy of her own fireside, where, while she sat and worked at the straw plait by which she earned her living, she would repeat passages of Scripture and verses from her favorite hymns, till the emotions kindled by the words gave a look almost of inspiration to her plain countenance.

It was strange that the only thing for which Martha's gentle heart cherished hatred was the Church of God, the spouse of Christ. "Do I not hate them that hate Thee!" she would murmur fervently as she mused on the evil deeds of this supposed enemy of Christ. Needless to say that it was a figment of her brain, or rather the inventions of those less innocent than herself, on which she expended her jealous hatred; and she proved its unreality by her distinct predilection for Catholic books of devotion when, it stands to reason, she did not know they were Catholic. In her small library no volume, next to her Bible, was so well thumbed as the "Imitation of Christ," shorn, as was the fashion some years ago, of its fourth book. The parson, an old-fashioned Evangelical, had been shocked by the sight of the volume on her table, and told her it was a Romish abomination. "Oh, no, sir," she replied with grave dignity, "I think you are mistook. It is all about the love of Christ and not a word about the Virgin Mary. Maybe, sir, you have not read it."—"Not I!" he replied; "but I know all about it, and take warning, my good woman, 'there's death in the pot!'"

Martha habitually resented any attempt either to interfere with her or offer her advice. She had no hesitation in considering her own opinion as her surest guide, and was, moreover, strongly possessed of the logically Protestant qualities of self-respect and proper pride, which among those outside are made to do the work of higher motives. Humility, with her sister Obedience, are virtues of which the Church still has the monopoly. But, on the other hand, Martha could give advice. She knew that she was held in high esteem by many of her neighbors, who considered her the best Christian in the place. She knew the position she held, and, without positive spiritual pride, accepted it, and, when others turned to her for advice, gave it, and thanked the Lord for having spoken to her.

It was, therefore, with no surprise that she received one November day a message that Florence Scott wished to see her at once. It is true that her countenance assumed a severe expression. She had led a blameless, perhaps untempted, life herself, and her horror of such sin as this girl's made her a little stern towards the sinner. Poor Florrie! hers was a sad story. Alas! it was no new thing in Appleton that girls should fall from the path of virtue, yet her fall created a sensation. Her parents were so well-to-do, and they and she had always held their heads so high, that something better was expected of her. Scott, the father, besides being the owner of about ten high-rented cottages, was a leading member of the Baptist community, and a preacher. As for the mother, she kept a maid-servant, and the lace mittens on her delicate hands proved that they were never soiled with manual work. Florence had been educated at a genteel boarding-school at L——; and when her so-called education was finished she had been placed in a millinery establishment in the same town. That was three years before this November afternoon, and she had held but slight communication with her family since. Then, a few weeks before, she had come home— and what a home-coming! The news of her shame and fall had been as a thunderbolt to her parents, and close on the news came the girl herself. She knocked at the door late one evening, and fell senseless across the threshold, and they could see she was dying. Even the sense of the disgrace she had brought on them could not make the Scotts turn her away, and now she lay awaiting death under their roof.

When Martha, accompanied by Mrs. Scott, entered Florrie's room, she could plainly see that the poor girl's days were numbered. "Martha," she said in a feverish whisper as soon as they were alone, "you're a good woman, I know, and care for people's souls more than anything else. For God's sake, Martha, go to B—— and fetch a priest to me."

"A priest, child, a Popish priest!" said Martha in astonishment. "But, Florrie girl, you're not a Papist?"

"I am, Martha, I am," the dying girl gasped.

"It was two years ago—but there, I have no strength to tell you how I became a Catholic. It was before all this sin and sorrow came on me, and I've never been nigh the church since. And now I'm dying; and before it is too late fetch me a priest."

But Martha set her lips tight. "I don't know how I could abet it," she replied. "Put your trust in the Lord Jesus, poor sinner. He is your salvation. Don't put your trust in Popish priests and mummeries." And, so saying, she knelt down by the bed and began to pray aloud.

"Oh, don't, Martha! What shall I do, what ever shall I do?" moaned poor Florence. "I thought you would have done it for me; and now God help me!" With a gasp the poor girl fell back, the blood streaming from her mouth.

As Martha raised her in her arms a feeling, strange to her, of diffidence in her own judgment came over her. She felt overpowered by the consciousness that she could make a mistake, and she felt herself trembling as she supported the sick girl. Who was she, an inner voice seemed to say, to set herself up and stand between a soul and its God? With sudden impulse she whispered to Florrie, "I'll do it for you," and, summoning Mrs. Scott to her daughter, she left the house like one in a dream.

The distance to B——, at which town the only Catholic church within reach stood, was five miles, and travelling was weary work, for the November day was drawing to its close and a drizzling rain was falling; and the thick clay soil of the lanes clung to Martha's boots, squeaking under her tread. But she heeded neither distance nor weather, and tramped along borne up by hidden excitement. She knew the way, for B—— was a market town, and the chapel was in the main street, so she went without loss of time to the door of the presbytery, and pulled the bell with beating heart.

"Is the Roman Catholic priest within?" she asked the stout and beaming housekeeper who answered her summons.

"What, Father Maple?" she replied. "Yes, he is in, and just finished his bit of dinner. You have a message for him? Please walk in and take a seat."

For the first time in her life Martha found herself standing face to face with that monster of iniquity —a Popish priest; but so mythical was the object of her detestation that she forgot to feel the fear and abhorrence which the occasion called for. She delivered her message simply, and, as briefly as she could, acquainted the priest with poor Florence's story, and then prepared to take her departure.

"Pray sit down, and let Mrs. Malony make you a cup of tea after your long walk," said Father Maple; but Martha refused his hospitality.

"No, sir, I thank you," she replied, with an inward feeling of repulsion to breaking bread under such a roof. "And to tell you the honest truth I had better get to Scott's before you, and be there when you arrive. They will be in a grand taking, and it's best I should be there. I've brought this on them, sir, and it's naught but right that I should be there to help. Once you get to the village you can't mistake the house, next to the inn at the cross-roads, standing in a bit of garden of its own. Good-evening, sir, and pray excuse me for troubling you on such a night." So saying she went off bravely, her holy angel and a quietly breathed prayer from the good priest accompanying her on the way.

Vague rumors of Florence's conversion had reached her parents' ears a twelvemonth before, but they refused to pay attention to them; and the girl's sad subsequent story and actual condition had driven the gossip from their mind. This afternoon, however, during Martha's absence Florence succeeded in breaking the truth to her mother; but, for prudence' sake, she said nothing about her friend's errand. Nor did that good woman feel bound to frustrate the object of her journey by confiding it to Mrs. Scott, who, she knew well, would never consent to admit a priest into her house, even were her dying child to drag herself out of bed and implore her on her knees. Martha felt doubtful whether Father Maple would succeed in effecting an entrance; nor would he have done so had not the hand of Providence smoothed the way.

By the time the priest arrived at Appleton the rain was coming down in sheets. He was clad in a long mackintosh, and a white muffler covered half his face, so that, though he had no intention to disguise himself, Mrs. Scott failed to recognize the nature of her visitor; and when he said that he had come to see her daughter, she quietly led him up-stairs, thinking he was the parish doctor's assistant. It was only when Florence tried to raise herself in bed and cried out: "Thank God, Father, you have come!" that the truth dawned upon her.

Then a scene took place in that chamber of death which would baffle description. The infuriated woman lost all control over her rage, and forgot all motherly feeling for the girl; and first calling shrilly to her husband, the preacher, to come to her assistance, she poured forth torrents of the foulest abuse on both the priest and her dying child. Never had she upbraided the latter for her sin as she upbraided her now; and it was apparent that she considered Florrie's conversion a far greater disgrace than her fall.

"O mother!" gasped poor Florence, as soon as there was a lull in the storm; "leave me. I want to go to confession and make my peace with God."

"Confession!" screeched the virago. "Not while I'm here will I let you do such devil's work." And Florrie, worn out, turned, sobbing silently, to Martha who stood by her side, ill at ease.

Meanwhile Preacher Scott, having washed himself at the sink and put on his best coat, appeared on the scene, and, at his wife's bidding, ordered Father Maple to leave the house, unless he wished him to fetch the village policeman. When the priest explained civilly and temperately exactly what Florrie wanted, both father and mother—he resolutely and she furiously—declared that they would stand by their daughter's bedside till she died rather than leave her alone to go to confession and sell herself to the devil. They evidently meant what they said; and Father Maple, seeing Florence's faint and exhausted condition, felt that no time was to be lost. So, leaning over her bed, he tried as best he could in the midst of the hubbub to explain that she must make an act of contrition and that he would give her conditional absolution. But the poor sinful girl, rousing her energies, cried out that she must and would make her confession, and, turning round, clung piteously to Martha Gray.

Again that crushing sense of her own fallibility came over Martha. As before, a sudden impulse seized her, and she turned on the foolish, chattering couple with a look of majesty and indignation. "Shame on you both," she said, "disturbing the poor thing's last moments like this, when she wants to prepare her soul to meet her God. It's not for you and me to say how she is to prepare. It's an awful moment for a soul, and each of us has got to do as God bids us." Then, suiting her actions to her words, she placed her hands first on the sleek preacher and then on his genteel wife, and, with muscular vigor, pushed them outside the door, against which she placed her back.

"There, sir," she said, breathing hard with the exertion and excitement, "there, let the poor girl do as she wishes. I'll not stand in her way."

"But we want you to leave us as well," said Father Maple, who could scarcely repress a smile at the situation. But Martha hesitated, and her countenance darkened.

"Well, well," she said after a pause. "I'll let be. Maybe all the things that people say are not true. I'll trust the poor dying thing to you, sir; and I'll see you're not disturbed." And taking up her post outside she stood like a watchful sentinel at the head of the stairs, though neither Mr. nor Mrs. Scott attempted any further interference.

At last Father Maple opened the door and called Martha in. "See to her, Mrs. Gray, will you?" said he. "And try to keep her last hours free from disturbance. I have done for her all that I can, but will come again if she should want me; but I do not, myself, think she will be here many hours. Will you send me a line to-morrow to tell me how she is?"

"I'll be sure to let you know how she does, sir,"

replied Martha, a sense of so-called self-respect forbidding her to tell Father Maple that, though long practice made reading easy to her, the construction of a letter was beyond her. "But," she added, "I fear me I have done a wrong thing by the poor girl this day."

"No, Mrs. Gray," replied the priest gravely, "you have done a good work by her—a work pleasing to God. As you know, our blessed Lord will not let the gift of even a cup of cold water pass unrewarded, so be sure you will get your reward. Good-night." So saying he went down-stairs, and, silently raising his hat to the sullen couple in the kitchen, passed out swiftly into the rain and darkness.

Martha slept but little that night. Her heart beat and her pulses throbbed with unwonted emotions. The face of her God was hidden from her as by a cloud; and as she tossed to and fro on her pillow, with prayer on her lips, she wondered whether she had sinned against Him by human compassion, and He had turned from her in anger. But through her prayers for pardon the priest's parting words rang in her ears, and again and again she seemed to hear the sentence of the Divine Judge: "Inasmuch as you have done it unto one of the least of these My brethren you have done it unto Me."

As soon as she had cooked and eaten her frugal breakfast Martha hastened to Florrie's bedside.

The parents were silent and sullen in their reception, though they did not try to stop her from going to the girl. But when she was half way up the stairs Mrs. Scott hissed out after her the word "Papist!" Poor Martha, to think that she should have lived to be called a Papist! If she had, unconsciously to herself, cherished a desire to question Florence, a glance showed her that the time for conversation was passed, and the girl lay, half-conscious and speechless, awaiting the last dread moment. But the look of absorbed rest and peace on her countenance could not fail to strike her visitor. A small crucifix lay near her helpless hand. It was the first that Martha had ever seen, and she tried to turn her eyes from it with abhorrence as an object of foolish idolatry; but, in spite of herself, tears of tenderness welled up in her eyes as she looked at the effigy of her dying Lord. Florrie saw the struggle and smiled faintly. "Oh, I am so happy!" she murmured. "How good you have been to me, Martha! Peace at last—all—all forgiven."

For some hours Martha sat by Florrie's bed, listening to her wanderings, till, with a last ray of coherence, the dying girl cried out, "Sweet Jesus, mercy!" and yielded up her spirit to Him. Martha was alone with her, praying on her knees, when she died. The parents, though mindful that their daughter should lack no necessary care, expressed their moral indignation at her conduct of the previous day by a studious avoidance of any sign of affection. So Martha closed her eyes, and, seeing the crucifix between her fingers, put it in her pocket with a nameless sense of reverence. It might be an object of idolatry, but none the less it represented Christ; and she could not leave it to be profaned, as she knew it would be, by the bigotry of the Scotts. Surely, the cups of cold water were multiplying in her hand.

"I said I'd tell him," muttered Martha to herself, as she sat over her early and solitary tea; "so I must." She sighed with weariness as she thought of the long, muddy tramp to B——. Her bad night and the emotions of the last twenty-four hours had worn her out; yet she would not flinch from what she considered a duty. But weary in very truth she was when she reached Father Maple's house; and she could have cried with vexation when, having knocked two or three times without response, she was convinced the house was untenanted.

"They're in yon," called out a little boy from the other side of the street, pointing as he spoke down a passage by the side of the presbytery. She walked down this with no thought beyond finding some one to whom to deliver her message; but almost before she knew where she was she found herself inside the Catholic chapel, the altar of which, though she knew it not, was prepared for Benediction. Some dozen people were already in the church, and several pairs of children's eyes gazed curiously at her. This confused her, and thinking that her exit might cause disturbance in a "place of worship," Martha made her way to the further end of one of the benches and sat down. Had a service been going on her conscience might have forbidden the action, but as it was she had no scruple. By the time the candles were lighted, and the priest and acolytes had filed in, many worshippers had crowded in, and Martha found herself absolutely hemmed into her seat. In a moment ever blessed to her she decided that the evil of staying where she was was less than that of forcing her way out.

Our blessed Lord has many ways of speaking to the souls of those who are willing to listen to Him; and, among the thousands who have accepted His invitation into the one fold, no two are led in precisely the same way. Some are converted through their reason, others through their emotions; some are convinced by Scripture, others by the facts of history. To some few Our Lady has appeared in vision, while to others—thrice-blessed they—Our Lord deigns to speak silently from the tabernacle in tones which, though voiceless, will take no refusal. Such was His blessed way with plain Martha Gray, who had been so faithful to Him according to the light given to her.

Who could attempt to describe what took place

in her soul? The secrets of God cannot be put into words; and she herself, when questioned later, could scarcely tell what happened to her. She never knew how or at what moment she fell on her knees and covered her face with her hands. She dared not stir, so strong was her realization of the presence of our blessed Lord; and she felt that had she raised her eyes she would have seen that which no man or woman could look on. She had no thought about the Blessed Sacrament; indeed she knew nothing about that mystery of mysteries beyond a vague and shuddering horror of what she had been taught to call the wafer-god of the Romanists.

Benediction was over, but Martha had scarcely found out that any service was going on. Before her shrouded eyes the ceremonies had passed unnoticed; and the hearty, discordant singing of the congregation had made no impression on ears which were listening to the voice of God. The subsequent silence was equally unperceived, and she knelt on in the church, alone with Him who had spoken to her heart.

About a quarter of an hour later Father Maple came in to lock up the chapel. Seeing a woman absorbed in prayer he was loath to disturb her; but he had a distant parishioner to visit that evening, and could not stand on ceremony, so, having fidgeted about and jangled his keys noisily without producing the desired effect, he touched her gently on the shoulder, thinking that she might have fallen asleep. "You, Mrs. Gray?" he exclaimed, as he recognized the startled face which met his gaze. "What brings you here?"

"I came to tell you as how Florrie was dead," she replied, passing her hand over her brow as though she were dazed, while she remained on her knees. "But oh, sir," she continued, "the Lord Jesus has been very nigh me."

"What?" said the priest softly, "and has the cup of cold water been rewarded already?"

"The Lord is in this place, and I knew it not," Martha went on, readily expressing herself in the words of Scripture. "Tell me, sir, is He here?"

"Yes, He is here," replied Father Maple, with an awe-struck feeling of gratitude, which all who live by faith must have when something approaching to sight is vouchsafed to them.

"The Lord is, I know, not far from every one of us," she continued, still speaking like one in a dream; "but is He nigher to us here in this place?" The priest silently bowed his head, and Martha went on: "I think what you say is the truth, sir. I know the Lord is always nigh. Day after day as I sat at my work I have known He was at hand, and night after night I have communed with Him on my bed; but never has He been nigh me as He has been in this place. Why, sir, I was afeared to raise my eyes lest I should meet His look. It was as if He was speaking to me, though, mind you, never a word did I hear. But oh, sir! I couldn't have met His look"—and here her voice shook and her lips quivered—"it was if He was displeased with me; as if He knew of something as I hadn't done for Him, and ought to have done."

The priest had seated himself on the bench in front of Martha, so that he could listen to her as she knelt; but he made no reply to her words, reserving what he had to say till the Holy Ghost had finished speaking to her; and after a pause she continued: "Sir, something has happened to me since I have been here. I feel like as if I had been struck to the ground as Paul was. I feel such a sinner, and I never knew it before. I know we must all be washed in the blood of the Lamb, but I thought the Lord had chosen and saved me. But as He stood by me just now, as I know He did, I felt like an unclean thing, and I know not where to find a Pool of Siloam in which I may wash and be clean. I know nothing. I thought I had been taught of God, but I know nothing, nothing. Sir"—she added, looking up in the priest's face with a quivering lip, which gave her the expression of a little child—"Sir, what shall I do?"

She had been speaking fluently and excitedly, but the sound of her own helpless question—the same that millions and millions of perplexed souls have uttered since it was first put to St. Peter by the conscience-stricken Jews—struck her ears, and she burst into silent weeping, with a sense of accepted humiliation which opened for her the golden gates of humility.

"Mrs. Gray," said the priest, seeing that the moment had come for him to speak, "you scarcely know yet how good God has been to you to-day; for you have no idea what God's gifts to men are."

"I'm very unlearn'd, sir," she said, in a voice broken by her tears. "Can I learn?"

"Yes, indeed, if you are willing. But would you consent to own that you have been in the wrong all your life?"

"I feel just shook, sir," was her reply. "I feel as if I was no better than a child; but I know the Lord Jesus requires somewhat of me."

"You say, Mrs. Gray," the priest continued, after lifting up his heart to God, "that when our blessed Lord was, as you felt, standing by you, He seemed to reproach you?"

"Ay, sir, it was just like that, and I've got to find out and do as He wants me."

"Perhaps," resumed Father Maple, "He meant to show you His sorrow that you should be contented to live without all those good things He died to give you."

Martha gripped the priest's arm almost painfully. "What are they, sir, that I may have them? I know nothing about them."

"Ah, Mrs. Gray," he said with a smile, "it would take a long, long time to tell you about all the wonderful things our blessed Lord left for His children when He went to heaven. It would take days and days to tell you about His holy Catholic Church which He left to teach us when He Himself was no longer here to speak to us. He charged her to take care of us all through our earthly pilgrimage, to forgive us our sins in His name, and feed our souls in a way I cannot tell you now."

"It makes the Lord very nigh," said Martha thoughtfully. "It seems as if we could stretch out our hands back all these long years, and touch Him."

"He is nigher than you can ever guess. Will you come back another day and hear more?"

"Ay, sir, sure I will," she replied with simple alacrity. "It seems just what was wanting." She now rose to her feet, and Father Maple could see that her eyes were full of happy tears. "I must not detain you longer to-night, for I've took up a lot of your time," she went on, with the habitual diffidence of those who have spent their lives in ministering to others and have never been ministered unto. "But be sure I'll come back and hear more about those gifts Our Lord Jesus left for us, if so be it will not be troubling you over much. Good-evening, sir, and thank you kindly."

It is scarcely necessary to give the sequel to the events of that evening. Suffice it to say that, eager to learn, and hungering for God's gifts, simple Martha Gray thought nothing of tramping day after day to B——, regardless of the rains and fogs of autumn or the frosts and snows of winter, and received the word of God into "a good and very good heart." As she learned more about the eternal mysteries, she could scarcely believe that such joy was meant for her. And when, at last, having been washed in the Pool of Siloam, she was admitted to the divine banquet, she said amid her gentle, happy tears, "It seems quite natural like." Her words, singularly inappropriate as they were for describing that which is so essentially and awfully supernatural, expressed to the best of her ability the readiness of her faithful, Christian soul to apprehend the highest mysteries of God, and the instinctive way in which it made its home in the Sacred Heart of Jesus. It was, indeed, as she had said, *just what was wanted.*

R. B. SHERIDAN KNOWLES.

R. B. SHERIDAN KNOWLES is the eldest and only surviving son of the late Richard Brinsley Knowles, a barrister, the author of "The Maiden Aunt," and a well-known London journalist. He is the grandson of James Sheridan Knowles, author of "Virginius," "The Hunchback," "The Love Chase," etc., and great-grandson of James Knowles. the lexicographer, whose mother, Hester Knowles, *née* Sheridan, was the daughter of Dr. Thomas Sheridan of Quilca, the friend of Swift, and grandfather of Richard Brinsley Sheridan. the author of "The School for Scandal."

R. B. Sheridan Knowles received his education at the college of the Rosminian Fathers. at Ratcliffe, in Leicestershire, and on the completion of his college course entered the Civil Service. His contributions to literature consist mainly of essays, sketches, and reviews, which have appeared in various journals and periodicals. His most recent, as also his most important work, is the novel " Glencoonoge," a story of Irish life, which having run serially for a year in *The Month*, was republished in three volumes by the famous Edinburgh house of Wm. Blackwood & Sons, and in one volume in America.

" Hyacinth's Regrets " has been written by Mr. Knowles specially for this collection.

Hyacinth's Regrets.

BY R. B. SHERIDAN KNOWLES.

I.

IF the heroine of this story was a very self-willed woman it may fairly be urged in her excuse that everything had combined to make her so. Probably she had more than her natural share of self-will by inheritance, for her parents—sober, industrious people—were both teetotallers, and you may have observed that that cult has a strengthening, not to say stubbornizing, effect upon the wills of those who practise it. Then, too, Hyacinth was an only child, and by consequence much prized and cherished by her parents, who kept her aloof from the companionship of other children of her own age; thus guarding the girl from the dangers of such companionship, and also from its educating and correcting influences. If this was the policy of John Smith and Emma his wife in regard to their child in those days, when their position was only lifted above that in which life was a struggle for existence by the practice of rigid economy, it is not to be supposed that their fastidiousness in regard to the manner of little Hyacinth's bringing-up should grow less as the bread-winner advanced from the position of first-counterman to being a shopkeeper on his own account, and then a merchant with a steadily growing connection. "Thank goodness," said they in effect, " fortune has favored us soon enough to make it unnecessary to send the girl to a boarding-school or convent, where the time is, as often as not, wasted, and girls are turned out with the merest smattering of education." Hyacinth had a governess all to herself, and the best masters; but none of them were able to master her. Her wishes, indeed, eventually decided everything —what she would learn, how much, and how long. Sometimes, no doubt, she was in the right, as when she struck against the singing and music lessons. The girl had no music in her, and it was sheer imposture on the part of Signor Pagano to declare that after another five-and-twenty, thirty, forty lessons (at a guinea each) the voice would begin to form, and both she and her friends would be astonished. The dismissal of the music-master made other professors very careful not to force or thwart the wishes of an only child.

I think that Hyacinth was the most graceful dancer I ever saw. In fact, the grace of her bearing and the appropriateness of her manner to every different occasion showed how thoroughly well drilled she had been in the matter of deportment. To see her coming down the nave with her people as the congregation filed out of church after High Mass on Sundays was a pleasure—so fresh she looked, so sweetly demure; her glances—rare and under perfect control—all bespoke a well-disciplined character. "She will make a good match," that was what every one said.

Well, young Aubrey Lushington's position was not bad socially. He was of the family of the Earls of Lushington, and to be allied to nobility is something, even though you may be only the younger son of a younger son, without a profession or visible means of subsistence. Hyacinth felt that these latter conditions were the drawbacks destined in her case to prevent the course of true love from running smooth. How often had she not heard her father pooh-pooh the exaggerated estimate in which she and her mother were disposed to hold birth and social position! If there had only been himself to please he would have left society and its fancies severely alone. But to his wife and daughter these things were as the breath of life, to the former by contrast with the poverty and dulness of her early circumstances, to the latter as the bud of promise which would presently expand into a brilliant future.

If evening parties were delightful at first for their own sake, what an added relish did they not possess when, having met Aubrey Lushington two or three times, Hyacinth began to feel that he was quite the nicest of all her partners, dancing so much better than any one else, and so much more interesting in his conversation between the dances. He had seen so much of life though he was so young. How clever he was! And you could perceive from the ease of his manner, and the polished readiness of his remarks, above all, from his marked deference to her, that he was of noble blood. Hyacinth and Aubrey became quite friendly, quite confidential; they knew of each other's engagements for weeks ahead; and by degrees the prospect of coming entertainments lost their attractiveness to Hyacinth if Aubrey was not going too. On these days Hyacinth would infallibly mope. But if it was an evening when Aubrey was to be of the party, what anxiety beforehand about the choice of the dress! what thought in the combination of colors, in the selection of flowers! and at night what cosy chats in the subdued light upon the stairs! what heavenly waltzings! what joyous suppers!

"My dear," said Mrs. Riddles to Mrs. Smith one day, "are you encouraging the growing intimacy between Hyacinth and young Mr. Lushington?"

Mrs. Smith had noticed something, but did not think there was anything serious in it—a little flirtation, nothing more. She did not wish, unless there was absolute need, to cross her daughter on the subject, she being a dear child, so sensitive and highly strung, that the very greatest care was necessary in finding the smallest fault with her.

Mrs. Riddles looked at Mrs. Smith incredulously. Then with a sudden burst—

"Everybody is talking of it. People say they are engaged—not that I thought it at all likely."

"I should think not, indeed," answered Mrs. Smith indignantly. "Why, the young man has no profession, and very little means."

"Has he any? I should be very much surprised if he is not heavily in debt. How can it be otherwise if he has no means and no profession? And leading a fast life, too!"

Mrs. Smith was horrified.

"Yes," continued the other, laughing. "Well, what else can you expect?—it runs in the family. His father was——" and she proceeded to relate to Mrs. Smith some of the Lushington family history in a whisper.

Mrs. Smith returned home in a state of consternation, revolving within herself how she might best restrain her daughter from walking into the unsuspected gulf which lay yawning before her.

If was an off night. Hyacinth and her mother were alone together in the drawing-room. Mrs. Smith uneasily eyed her daughter, who sat looking into the fire, somewhat discontented because they were not going anywhere.

"Hyacinth, do you care for young Mr. Lushington?"

The girl was taken by surprise, and after a moment's reflection answered with somewhat bated breath :

"I like him as a partner, he dances beautifully."

The mother was silent for a few moments and then said:

"Hyacinth——" and then stopped.

"Well, mother?" said the breathless girl.

"He would not make a good partner for life. You are dancing too much with him. People are beginning to talk."

"I wish people would attend to their own affairs. What right have they to talk about what does not concern them?"

"People will talk if you give them the chance, or even without a chance."

"What do they say of him, mother?"

"They say that he leads an idle life—and—and a wild life. Do not seek to inquire too closely; there is more evil in the world than it is necessary for you to know of yet."

"Ah, mother, believe me he is not blind to his own faults. He has bewailed them to me. He says he has no one to care for him, and that he will never be what he ought to be until he is married to some good girl. I am sure," added Hyacinth, with suddenly assumed indifference, "I wish he could find such a one. I don't know what nobler mission a girl can have than to reform a man."

"Indeed," said the mother, suppressing any manifestation of her alarm, now thoroughly aroused, "reformation is much needed in that quarter."

That night Mrs. Smith opened her mind to her husband. He blamed her for having been so blind to what had been going forward, and yet he was more good-humored over the matter than she had expected.

"It is strange," said he, "that I should hear about this on the very day when what I have been desiring for many months past should suddenly have happened. This afternoon, as I was about to leave the warehouse, who should come in but young Fergusson. From his nervousness I half-guessed what he was after. I was right, too. He has proposed for Hyacinth."

"Thank goodness! This will help us out of the difficulty, I hope."

"I could not desire a better husband for the girl. In fact, I had set my heart upon it—and so, it seems, had he. He had just been offered—what do you think?"

"I cannot guess," said Mrs. Smith, overjoyed.

"A junior partnership in his firm, and the first thing he does is to come like a man and ask to be allowed to share his good fortune with our girl. A sterling fellow! I always liked him. I picked him out from all the men I knew and said, '*That's the man I should like to ask me for my Cythie.*' And she captivated him, the little wench—though she didn't know it. And I don't know that she deserves him, if she can think of throwing herself away on a creature like young Lushington. What are you going to do about him? He must never be asked here again, of course."

"Oh, no! Nor will we go again anywhere this season where she will be likely to meet him. But say nothing of all this to Hyacinth. I do think she is more perverse than most girls, and there is no telling what she will do if she is openly thwarted."

II.

They were very astute, these people, but they underrated the intelligence of the young thing whose future they were designing to shape. Nothing, indeed, was said: but when at dinner next evening Mr. Smith was full of the sudden good-fortune which had befallen Mr. Fergusson and enlarged upon it with much gusto, and said that Mr. Fergusson was coming to dinner the following evening and they would hear more; and when two days later, being due that evening at Lady Lyster's, where Aubrey was to have been, Mrs. Smith told Hyacinth that Mr. Fergusson had very kindly invited them to dine at the Criterion, and to go with him to the opera afterwards; and they would go there in preference to the Lysters', as dear papa would never go to dances, and he enjoyed dinners above all things, and she was afraid they had been leaving him too much alone lately; and then Mr.

Fergusson was very attentive and continually the only gentleman of the party, and upon occasion after occasion some glib reason or another was given why the engagement to the house where Aubrey was to be was suspended in favor of one at which Mr. Fergusson was to be either the guest or the host (whether as host or as guest he was equally attentive—and equally detestable, Hyacinth thought), Hyacinth, though nothing was said, understood, and said—nothing. She disguised her thoughts under the placid expression of face she knew how to assume, but the thought in her mind was, " I'll let them see whether or not I'm going to be treated as a child."

It gave Mrs. Smith great pleasure to observe her tranquil and submissive behavior, and also to notice that the girl showed signs of becoming devout. It had never been Hyacinth's habit to attend afternoon service, until it happened just at this time that her mother, seeing her one day quite distressed with ennui, and hearing the church-bell ringing, said, " Do, my child, cultivate a spirit of self-denial and go to Rosary "—a suggestion which to her surprise the girl eagerly caught at. And what was more, Hyacinth kept the practice up. It was quite usual for Hyacinth after that to say, yawning wearily, " Ach ! I want a walk. I think I'll just stroll round to church." Until Mr. Fergusson had begun to come so much, and with intentions hardly to be mistaken, the girl had never betrayed so much seriousness. Mrs. Smith was delighted. She thought it a good sign, an evidence, in fact, that Hyacinth was seeking the illumination of Heaven in deciding the momentous question of her marriage.

Mrs. Smith's haphazard suggestion had indeed been a light to Hyacinth's mind in her perplexity to checkmate the combination which was keeping her from meeting Aubrey Lushington. The service-hour was now usually spent by her in company with Aubrey in a first-class carriage of a circle train on the underground railway. There they exchanged indignant sympathy; there they vowed that nothing should ever part them; there they matured their plans.

Elated with her success and Aubrey's devotedness, Hyacinth became more and more good-tempered, and the better tempered she was, the more pleased were her father and mother with her. But their approval was pulled up very short a little later when, in the calmest but most conclusive manner possible, she declined Mr. Fergusson's proposal. Her conduct was altogether unaccountable, until it came out that her affections were already engaged, and to Aubrey Lushington. It was in a quiet conversation with her mother, who, after some deft probing, had extracted the truth. Mrs. Smith told her daughter the worst things she had heard about Aubrey; Mr. Smith said he would horsewhip the young man if he dared to come near the house; both were agreed that they would rather see her dead than married to such a man. This last was the reply to her argument that all men worthy of the name were a little wild at first before they settled down, and everybody said such always made the best husbands. Stubborn-willed as Hyacinth was, she began to have misgivings that she was acting rashly; that in this matter her parents would be as stubborn as herself, and that she would never gain their consent. Had it not been for Aubrey's encouragement she had perhaps given way. But he gauged the situation pretty accurately, perceiving that Mr. Smith was not the kind of man who would forever refuse to forgive his only child, however erring; and that the mother's influence would confirm his natural tendency to relent. He did not say so to Hyacinth. To her the purport of his remarks ran thus: "My father will help us, Cythie, if yours won't; he has influence; he will get me an appointment. I ask for nothing but yourself, dearest; I am content with poverty if I have you, for in you is all my happiness, my one chance of salvation."

"Noble fellow," thought Hyacinth, as she thought and rethought over these words, "shall I refuse to save him? Can I hesitate longer to grasp his drowning hand held out to me for succor?"

Some little time passed and then it was discovered that Hyacinth was meeting Aubrey

Lushington clandestinely. To her parents' reproaches she uttered not a word. She was desired to withdraw to her room and think the matter over. And in her absence her father and mother considered what was to be done. They would adjure her at least not to act precipitately: and in the mean time she must be taken abroad out of reach of this danger—and at once, before she could communicate again with Aubrey. Time might thus be gained, and the infatuation have a chance of wearing off. This conclusion arrived at, Mrs. Smith followed her daughter up-stairs. Hyacinth was not in her room. An instinctive alarm seized the mother. She went hurriedly from room to room and from floor to floor, calling, but receiving no answer. In descending the stairs Mrs. Smith saw that the hall-door was slightly ajar, she stood beside it petrified, but perfectly collected. After looking up and down the street she went up-stairs to her husband.

"I am afraid Hyacinth has left the house," she said quietly.

The father started up. "Impossible!"

"I have hunted high and low; and just now found the hall-door half open."

The two stood looking at each other, both pale, and neither daring to utter the thought that was in both their minds.

"Perhaps she has gone to church," said Mrs.

Smith, clutching at an inspiration that had just occurred to her.

"We will take a hansom," said Mr. Smith. "Do you know where—where *he* lives?"

"No; but Lady Lyster perhaps can tell us."

They drove to the church. The windows were dark, the doors closed, there was no service that night.

Then to Lady Lyster's. She was gone out.

Another friend, however, had the name of Aubrey's club in her address-book. Thither they drove. He had been there that afternoon, but was not there now. His private address? The secretary had left for the day. It could not be furnished.

What were they to do? Perhaps she had returned home. But when they got there—no, she had not come back.

Those two people sat up the whole night waiting—silent for the most part. They could not see their way to immediate further action. Suggestions arose to their minds only to be seen to be futile as soon as uttered. What a night! In it they experienced, as it were, the crumbling into utter ruin of all the results of their self-abnegation, and the success of their lives. A horrible certainty was in their minds: they were disgraced forever and ever; never again would they be able to hold up their heads; life would be no more worth living, nor further strivings of any avail.

The longest night wears away. The morning came, and, late in the long morning, the knowledge of the truth. The postman was the messenger of fate. They heard his rat-tat coming down the street; the wretched father and mother waited in the hall with the letter-box unlocked. A packet fell on the floor, preceding the double knock. They hurried into the dining-room and shut the door. There were two documents in the envelope, a letter and—oh, welcome sight!—a marriage certificate.

III.

AUBREY and Hyacinth had been married for a fortnight. The astonishing news, if received a few hours before, would have been accounted disastrous; now it was actually as welcome as a reprieve to a condemned man. Compared with the possibility which had been in their minds the whole of that long night, it seemed as if everything was gained in receiving this assurance that the girl's honor was saved. Yet presently the first glow of this feeling began to fade, and as the facts came out, much of their anger against their child returned, mixed with and checked by gloomy forebodings for her future. Aubrey and Hyacinth had been married at the registry office. Hyacinth begged her parents' forgiveness. She was terrified, she said, by an indefinite fear of what was going to happen. Knowing what she did, their cold anger at discovering that she had been meeting Aubrey had made her too frightened to tell them face to face that she was already married to him; and in her scare she could think of no course but to fly to her husband.

Though somewhat revived, both father and mother were quite downcast. Married at the registry office! without the blessing of the Church! the sacraments unapproached, the aid of God unasked!

Well! at least the worst was escaped. The girl was not ruined, nor were they hopelessly disgraced in their old age. Other things might be retrieved. They would summon up what heart they could, and set to work to make the best of things.

There were not wanting elements of hope in the situation. Aubrey had a very taking manner with him when he chose, and Mr. Smith's spirits began to be raised after a time by the readiness with which his son-in-law fell in with his proposals. The merchant decided to take Aubrey into his office and give him a chance of learning the business. He would allow the pair only a moderate income; for the young man must be stimulated in his exertions by the thought that advancement into easier circumstances lay in his own hands. For the present he must work with nose to the grindstone; society and its pastimes must be eschewed for the most part. Mr. Smith had further designs at the back of his head which he thought it best not as yet to divulge, until he should see what aptitude for business and what perseverance the young man might display; but his hope was that Aubrey would show steadiness and capacity enough to justify his being taken later on into partnership, and become in time the inheritor of the business—a reasonable arrangement enough, seeing that the merchant had no son of his own.

Though Mr. Smith said nothing of his projects, the expediency and probability of such a result suggested itself at once to both the young people. Aubrey, indeed, thought it so obvious and inevitable that he rather pooh-poohed the anxiety of Hyacinth, who was very desirous that Aubrey should justify her choice of him. In truth, Hyacinth's anxiety was warranted, as Aubrey had everything to learn; and it presently became terribly tedious to this man, who had always been an idler, to live without the gayety of the life to which he was accustomed, and spend monotonous evenings in supplying the defects of training which stood in the way of his properly devoting wearisome days to the vulgarity of a mercantile life. As time went on he grew more and more restive under his fetters, and often wished that he had either never seen Hyacinth, or that she had had her money before he married her.

At the end of a year he was no longer the person of the first importance in that small household, but another bearing his name. To Hyacinth nursing her child, life presented itself in a new and more responsible aspect, and thinking now of her son, and hardly any longer of herself, she would sit ruminating and forecasting in his behoof. One day, if Aubrey did as well as he ought to, this child would inherit her father's business, and she began to take a keener and more pressing interest regarding the chances of Aubrey's proving fit to preserve and to transmit the business to their son.

So it was doubly galling to find from what her mother said, and from her father's lessened friendliness with Aubrey whenever they now went home, that things were not going well at the office. But when she broached the subject—of utmost importance in her mind—Aubrey would turn crusty. He had had enough of badgering and faultfinding during the day, and, after a few times, when he found Hyacinth drifting towards her favorite topic he would put his foot down.

His refusal to discuss and be interested in a topic which had become almost more interesting to Hyacinth than any other led to repeated disagreements which left the one dogged and the other sullen, and made evenings at home anything but pleasant.

Hyacinth would go to her father's.

Aubrey would put on his hat and go for a walk.

It was often late before Aubrey got home. Hyacinth had gone to bed. What did she care?

Before long it happened sometimes that Aubrey did not come home all night.

Hyacinth would now sit up and wait for Aubrey, enduring much. If she lay down, her tortured mind would not let her sleep. Self-reproach was busy at her ear.

"You married this man with your eyes open," it said. "You were warned that he was a spendthrift, leading a bad life, without occupation or means, coming, too, from a bad stock. If things have gone wrong with him you may thank yourself, partly for a mistaken choice obstinately persisted in, partly for the want of good-tempered management, by which you have driven him back to his former courses."

Hyacinth lived all that time of her courtship over again. Everything that had been sweet was turned to gall in the retrospect. "Heavens," she would exclaim, "did any woman ever before make such shipwreck of her happiness!" One thing was certain, they must part. Better the lonely home, better solitude with her child, than live with her husband any longer. Even consideration for the child did not come in here to keep the parents together. Aubrey did not care for the boy. Hyacinth felt that contact with the father would be contamination to the child. Separation was imperative. Aubrey had furnished abundant cause. There was no lack of money to carry through the necessary legalities; and in this matter, too, Hyacinth had her own way.

IV.

It is some years later. Mrs. Smith is dead, and Hyacinth keeps house for her father, who has aged more than might have been expected in an interval not very long. The failure of Aubrey Lushington to rise to the opportunities which his marriage brought him, and the decline of Mr. Smith's own health, have made the latter anxious for some time past to enter into arrangements which shall relieve him on advantageous terms of the sole responsibility of his business. His desire has just been obtained, thanks to the co-operation of that very Mr. Fergusson whose ambition it had been formerly to become his son-in-law. "A strange thing it is," ruminated Mr. Smith, "that my designs, blown to fragments by the perversity of my unfortunate girl, should after all these years be partly realized. It would be stranger still, it would be inconceivably happy, if after so long a delay they should be carried out as fully as I had once intended. I should die happy. Poor Emma! My delight would have only one drawback—that she did not live to see the realization of our dreams!"

Thenceforth the firms of John Smith & Co. and Davids, Beale & Fergusson (in the latter Mr. Fergusson was now the sole surviving principal) were known under the style and title of Smith & Fergusson; and it was in connection with this renewed community of interests that Mr. Fergusson became once more an occasional visitor at the home of his own old friend.

It was not very long before Hyacinth, regarding the visitor with eyes now disillusioned, began to perceive what a chance of happiness she had wilfully thrown away. That apparent coldness, hardness, and stolidity which had seemed so unattractive when contrasted with the lightness, brightness, and abandon of Aubrey's manner now seemed to be only so much trustworthiness—the one thing, as she now thought, to be desired above all others. It would have been no unhappy fate, she felt, to have been allied to a character stronger than her own—strong and prudent as this man's. It is good, thought she, for a child when he has such a father.

For her boy, whom she loved far more than anything else in the world, caused her no little anxiety. At times he was as good as gold, and then she could not fondle him enough. At others he made her very unhappy, and she was at her wits' ends to know what to do with him. She would coax him into good behavior; she would promise him things, and bribe him to be good—feeling all the time that this was not the right way nor for the boy's benefit. And often in her perplexity how to treat the boy she would think that the solution of her difficulties would have been easy if she had married Mr. Fergusson instead of the other.

And then how true Mr. Fergusson had been to his first love! It gave her real pleasure to remember that in all the seven years that had passed he had never married. People often said he would die an old bachelor, and involuntarily the words would escape as they looked at her. "What a pity, my dear, what a pity!" Meaning that it was clear she was the only woman he had ever cared for, and that she had thrown herself away. Ah! no one knew the pity of it better than she did; and yet there was some comfort, too, in the fact that Mr. Fergusson had never married.

She never met her husband now, and in the most imaginative of her thoughts the possibility of their ever coming together again did not present itself Sometimes she heard of him, but the disdain in her demeanor when his name was mentioned was not an encouragement to any one to speak about him. But one day some one said, "You have heard, of course, how ill your husband has been. No? They say he is a perfect wreck." Hyacinth was interested at once, and eagerly heard all that day that there was to be told. Not that she adopted the suggestion that she should go to see him. How could she—and would he be willing either—now that he had contracted other ties? But the news of his illness did not depress her, and she thought more often and with more gratitude how faithful Fergusson had been to his first love.

This constant thought enlightened her about

many things. It explained why it was that Mr. Fergusson was so respectful and so careful in his demeanor. Loving her as he still did, he would not for the world suggest by his manner that it was possible for her, a married woman, to return his love. " How like him!" she would think, not unpleased, " How noble! how like him!"

Mr. Fergusson grew to be so much in Hyacinth's thoughts that it was as it were by a sort of inevitable attraction that one day when she had opened the paper her eye fell straight and at once upon his name in a column of miscellaneous news. She began eagerly to read, and suddenly her heart stopped still. She turned pale and laid the paper down, hardly able to breathe. Was it the deaths column her eye had fallen upon? Was it the announcement of the death of her husband?

When she had recovered she took the paper up again and read the announcement through—of the forthcoming marriage of James Fergusson, Esq., of the firm of Smith & Fergusson, in the City of London, to Lady Gwendoline Acres, the youngest daughter of the Earl of Acres.

Irrevocably lost! So sharp a pang shot through her and was succeeded by such a heaviness of spirit that she awoke startled and humiliated, to perceive to how great an extent the thought had been in her mind that the mistake she had made years ago might one day be repaired, and how much it had been the source of her increased cheerfulness lately.

Stealing a glance at her father, she observed that his head was resting on his hand which was shading his eyes, and his attitude suggested some dejection.

"Is anything the matter, father?"

Mr. Smith suddenly came to himself and said:

"Nothing—nothing," then taking up a letter which was beside him he tossed it over, saying, "There's a bit of unexpected news."

It was a short note from Mr. Fergusson announcing his engagement. Mr. Smith watched his daughter while she read.

"So your old flame has been consoled at last. Those people didn't let the grass grow under their feet before they announced it in the papers. Having caught their fish I suppose they don't intend to let him slip—and they're wise. Ah! my girl, you might have had him once. You let a prize slip there. But," he added with the resignation of a man growing old and tired of fighting with fate, "there's no use in talking. What's done can't be undone."

He got up and went away, and the matter was not referred to again by either. It was more tolerable so. Hyacinth's feelings on the subject were too keen to be able to endure the most distant reference to it. She avoided meeting anybody who would be likely to speak of it, and became for a time something of a recluse; which perhaps lessened her humiliation, but not the poignancy of her grief, which could find only the relief afforded by secret, hopeless sighs and tears.

V.

About a year after Mr. Fergusson's marriage Mrs. Lushington became a widow. The circumstance affected her but little; her freedom now availed her nothing. Her father's death, however, when it happened a few years later, made a great difference, cutting her quite adrift from early associations and the anchorage of her life. It nipped her very near, too, in the disappointment and sense of slight she felt at finding that she was only to have a life interest in his property, which was secured to her son under the trusteeship of Mr. Fergusson. Should young Aubrey die she was to have absolute control over everything. But this proviso by no means reconciled her to the implied reproach contained in the terms of her father's will; and that irrevocable testament must always remain to perpetuate the slight feeling of estrangement it had created. Besides, the condition of her son's death was one which deprived the prospect of acquiring the full disposal of her inheritance of all attraction. If any doubt on this point had existed in any one's mind it would have been laid to rest when about his twelfth year young Aubrey fell a victim to mortal illness.

The boy had always been delicate, and the doctors looked serious. Mrs. Lushington was beside herself. For the first time in her life she was moved to the depths of her soul, and being so moved she sought for aid there where people turn when there seems no earthly hope left. She visited churches, she had Masses said, she made vows, she put abundant alms in the poor-box—that the boy's life might be spared. One day there was a consultation, and the doctors told her that she must prepare for the worst. When they were gone, she threw herself upon her knees and adjured God that He would spare her her son. He was the only thing she had. Life without him would be worse than death. "Anything, O God! anything but that!" Everything else she would endure gladly, suffer any loss or privation, give up all else, if only her child was left to her.

The doctors could not make it out. The disease did not take the turn they had thought inevitable; and slowly they began to take a less gloomy view. Even their modified forebodings were belied; for the boy recovered and did not bear the traces they had prophesied. What joy was not the mother's as young Aubrey progressed with slow but almost uninterruptedly continuous advance towards recovery! What were now her former regrets, her previous mistakes! Cobwebs, which this threatened sorrow and this anxious joy had swept out of remembrance. Never should those things she had pined for take possession of her again. This great sorrow had carried her far ahead, leaving the old days and the old life far behind and grown small in the distance. The future now! For her the future, her boy's future; in him were all her hopes; for him alone would she live. Hardly would she let him out of her sight. How dreary was one half-day without him! Besides, his escape had been too narrow for her to trust him out of reach of her careful watching. Aubrey had the best masters, the most careful professional training at home. What though he did not take kindly to studies, what if her ambitious hopes were being continually clouded by his want of application. Had she not promised that she would bear anything else if only she were not deprived of him?

It happened more than once that Mrs. Lushington as she looked at her son felt something like a stab at seeing how like he was, just that moment, to his father. But the next instant as he changed his position the likeness had vanished, and she had shaken herself free of the omen which had scared her.

The recollection of the danger in the past which she had escaped, the uncertainty and occasional suggestions of evil that might be in store for her in the future, made her at this time fairly contented with things as they were. But she never fully realized how happy these days had been until later on when she looked back on them. In the interval her boy, who had been all her own, her constant companion, whose studies she had shared, studying harder than he that she might make his task easier, who had always gone with her to church, who had been content to take no amusement but what she could share in, has grown up, has developed a taste for freedom, a disposition to live his own life, to choose his own friends, and go his own way.

Mrs. Lushington now passes many hours alone, brooding over her loss of influence over the young man, wondering where he is, what he is doing and in whose company; when he will come home; and whether he will ever again be to her as he was before. He does not talk freely and openly about himself and his doings. The friends he brings to the house she does not like, and tells him so. He does not bring them again, and is less often at home. As time passes she comes to be aware by degrees and by various means that Aubrey drinks, that he gambles, that he is leading a fast life.

Often in her long solitary vigils, angry and disappointed, her mind would go back to the time when, as a boy, his life was in danger; and she would remember her own anguish and how she had taken Heaven by storm, as it were, demanding and receiving her son's life. Would she have been quite so clamorous, she wondered, if she could have foreseen that it was only for this, after all, that she was asking?

A friend to whom she confided her grief said: "My dear Mrs. Lushington, you take the matter too seriously. It is of course very sad, and I do so sympathize with you. But Aubrey is no exception. Look at most of our young men who are good for anything, how wild they are at first. Look at most of our old men who have attained to any sort of eminence, have they not generally in their time sown wild oats? We must not make too much of these things. If others have come out without much permanent damage from such a life as Aubrey is leading, why should not he, in course of time? Depend upon it, you will see him a steady, sober, family man yet."

Mrs. Lushington extracted what comfort she could out of these reflections; but they did not afford her much. Aubrey could never again be the innocent boy she had worshipped and caressed. Whatever might hereafter come, she never could forget that he had preferred all and sundry to her, that he had been completely indifferent to her happiness, while he went away and enjoyed himself in all sorts of disreputable ways. Nor was his company when he bestowed it much of a pleasure now. He pestered her for money, and at length she found herself becoming straitened. Besides, by supplying him with the sinews of war was she not helping him to continue in his evil courses? She would not do it; and there followed pleadings and refusals, arguments and counter-arguments between mother and son. One day he left the house in a rage vowing he would never return. Hyacinth pulled herself together, hardened herself, declared that she was not going to give in to threats; did not shed a single tear, said she would no longer sit down and fret and pine away her life. There and then she ordered the carriage, dressed with unusual care, and drove out and made some calls. At the root of this strength was the knowledge that, not having the means to keep long away from her, Aubrey must sooner or later—probably sooner—return home. But when days passed, when weeks passed and he did not return, all her strength oozed away, and she could bear to remain in ignorance of his proceedings no longer. She employed a detective, and a pretty tale the detective brought her. He was enjoying himself at Margate with a ballet-girl from the Empire. He was very flush of money. How does he come by it? Why, the young gentleman has plenty of money, has he not? No? The detective was puzzled. He dismissed Mrs. Lushington's suggestion that the ballet-girl supplied the money with an easy "Not likely;" and later on returned more fully informed. Aubrey had realized his expectations. "And I should think, ma'am, at a great sacrifice, if it's true, as you say, that his expectations are dependent on the length of your life."

"It would have been better," this was the constant and bitter thought arising out of all Mrs. Lushington's cogitations—"it would have been better if he had died that time."

VI.

It goes without saying that young Aubrey had realized his expectations at a heavy loss. The idiot would agree to any proposal without understanding it, and sign any paper without reading it, if only the signature were to be followed by an advance of money. His financial agents reckoned him "good business," and having secured the reversion of his property at his mother's death, at ridiculous terms, they proceeded to try and obtain an immediate return for a further outlay by working upon the mother's affection for her son and her probable dread of his exposure to public shame.

When Mrs. Lushington understood the situation, how thankful she became, and how grateful to her father, till now somewhat estranged in death by reason of that will, for not making her absolutely his heir, for having placed his property under the trusteeship of a strong and honest man. Had the matter rested with her could she have refused to save her son from ignominy? Could she have withstood the machinations of those bloodsuckers? She knew she must have given way; she would have given up everything, and beggared herself. But now she had not the power. Nor had her trustee. Mr. Fergusson's advice was that there was only one way—a painful one—to free young Aubrey and his property from the money-lenders' clutches; and that was that, having been so mercilessly fleeced, he should take the offensive. No judge or jury would confirm the arrangements to which he had been practically a defrauded party. Mr. Fergusson's forecasts were fully justified by the result. But through what a sea—of anxiety on the part of the mother, of shame on the part of both mother and son—was it not through which they had to pass! The trial over, indeed, the revulsion of feeling in joy at success made Mrs. Lushington forget nearly all her trouble. Aubrey's inheritance was saved! It would be possible within a few years to free him entirely from liabilities. Mrs. Lushington was quite hopeful; and if anything could have put spirit into Aubrey it would have been his mother's astonishing display of light-heartedness. But the verdict did not rouse Aubrey from the depth of depression into which he had fallen during the protracted trial. Many things had come out of which he had thought but little previously; but which now, seen as it were from the point of view of other people's eyes, overwhelmed him with shame. To have caused so unsavory a sensation in society! To be the talk and reprobation of high and low, in private conversation and in the public press—all this overwhelmed him. He had no happiness by day, nor sleep by night. His mind, probably never well balanced, gave way under the strain of constant silent brooding and sleeplessness. One night in a fit of uncontrollable longing to put an end to his trouble the unfortunate lad sprang out of bed, tore open a drawer, snatched up a loaded revolver he kept there, and, putting the barrel in his mouth, blew out his brains.

VII.

This white-haired lady in black, slowly and painfully making her way along the silent street—is it possible it can be Mrs. Lushington? It is none other. Her head is bent. She has no eyes for the chance passer-by; she is possessed by her thoughts, and these forever harp on the same string. Where is her boy? She knows he is dead, it is not that so much which troubles her, as it is the torturing question. "Where is he now?"

This thought had flashed across her mind immediately upon the catastrophe. But the shock had then been too sudden and horrible, the rush of succeeding events too rapid, to let its slow, iterating, maddening effect be at first fully felt. Just as a drowning man grasps at a straw, so at that time Mrs. Lushington's whole eagerness had been to prove that Aubrey had all along been out of his mind. The verdict of suicide while temporarily insane seemed to her at first a verdict as it were of salvation for her son's soul. It was not she alone that thought it, she argued; twelve men unbiassed by interest or affection, having weighed all the evidence, had come to the same conclusion; and for a time that thought mitigated somewhat the cruellest part of her suffering. But when all was over, when Aubrey had been laid in the ground, and now eventless days followed one the other, all full for her of the same, monotonous, wearing thought, the scant comfort she had grasped at failed her utterly, and she sank prostrate in mind and body. She thought the hand of death was upon her, and death would have been welcome. But it was not to be.

Behold her, then, wasted to a shadow, suddenly aged, grown bent, white-haired, and strange, as she makes her way from the cottage in which she has taken a couple of rooms to be near the cemetery where Aubrey is buried; for to haunt his grave, to sit and pray there for long hours and lay her face upon the earth and call down to him, is her only solace.

As in fever the patient turns wearily from side to side in search of rest, trying again this posture and again the other, though before the change brought no relief, so does this poor lady seek consolation and advice from this quarter and from that, pouring out again and again the story of her misery and ask for guidance. Over and over again she has been admonished not to abandon herself to despair; to hope for her son in the mercy of God; and in her boy's name, and for him, to resign herself completely to the Divine Will. She tries to—it is all she can do. But it brings her but little comfort, and there are times when it affords her none.

One day she was returning in this despairing

frame of mind from the cemetery when, just as she was passing a church, a number of boys who had been chasing each other gathered panting about the open doorway, where they stood for a moment on the steps to recover breath and let their noisy laughter die down before going in. One of these boys at once attracted her attention, because of something about him which reminded her strongly of Aubrey. While she stool gazing, the youths with one accord crowded into the church and clattered up to the top benches of the nave; and Mrs. Lushington, eager for further sight of the lad, presently flitted like a shadow up one of the aisles to a seat in which she, unobserved, watched the group, and soon discovered that one in whom she was interested. It was an afternoon class for catechism for boys about to make their First Communion. It seemed as if in putting the questions the priest was going over ground in which instruction had already been given, to see if they had retained the substance of the previous lecture; for his questions, at least at first, were put without any obvious sequence or apparent connection with the main subject in hand. Mrs. Lushington was not listening to the questions at all, but sitting with her eyes fixed on the boy so like her son, and the mere looking at whom filled her with a bitter-sweet satisfaction. Suddenly the boy stood up. He had been addressed, but had not caught the question. The priest repeated it.

"May we ever feel sure concerning any person now departed out of this life, that he or she is in hell?"

"No, Father," answered the boy.

"Not if all the circumstances of his life and death point to his having died in mortal sin?"

"No, Father," answered the boy stoutly.

"Why not?"

"Because we do not know as much as God knows, and therefore we do not know what God's judgment is."

"Quite right. Now, what for instance do we not know?"

"We do not know," answered the boy that was like Aubrey, "how far the person may have been accountable for his actions."

"Exactly," said the priest; "therefore we can never be certain of any particular person that he or she is damned. And suppose," he went on, "that we have some one belonging to us who has died without a priest, without the sacraments, and apparently under circumstances which would at the first glance lead us to suppose that person to be lost, should we give up all hope of his salvation?"

"No."

"What should we do?"

"Pray and have prayers said for him."

"Anything else?"

"Do good works for him."

"Why?"

"Because by these means we may help him," answered the lad, and then, his questioning finished, sat down.

It seemed to Mrs. Lushington during this dialogue as if hers was the questioning mind, and that it was Aubrey's voice that was answering her. The voice and all it had said echoed in her ears long after the boys had left the church and had scattered in all directions. Its spell was upon her still when she reached home; and in the wakeful silence of the night it seemed to call out to her and say, "Mother, help me!"

It was the constant cry of that voice which first roused Mrs. Lushington and led her little by little back to life and into new activities, in which her wealth makes her a potent influence. Her mental horizon has become enlarged, and in seeing occasionally evidences of the good she is doing she experiences momentary thrills of exquisite happiness in feeling that she may be benefiting her son. A calm and sense of peace within herself are often hers to an extent which she hardly awhile ago would have believed possible. But sometimes the keenness of her great sorrow, with all its anguish and despair, regains for a time its mastery; and under the torture of its grip she cries out: "Oh, if only my poor boy had died that time, in his youth and innocence!"

FRANCES M. MAITLAND.

FRANCES MARY MAITLAND is one of a large family, and was brought up in a Scotch manse. While her father was proud of the old Presbyterian stock of which he came, her mother's people were Episcopalians and on one side Jacobite.

The happiest hours of Miss Maitland's existence were spent with the grandmother whose great-grandfather had laid down his life on Tower-Hill for the "Old Pretender," and whose uncle, with his own lips, had told her, many a time, of his visit to Prince Charlie at Rome.

Miss Maitland and her sister had English governesses to

improve their brogue. The first was dismissed because of her generosity in h's, the next, who had been brought up as a public singer and had lost her voice, knew little and taught less, and was at her happiest, her feet on the fender and a novel in her hand. The children did not like her on principle, for were they not brought up on Sir Walter's "Tales of a Grandfather," and was she not a Southern—one of the hereditary foes of their nation?

Their mother was delicate, and when her daughters grew up it was their grandmother who took the girls about, and enjoyed the fun just as heartily as they did.

Then came the death of Miss Maitland's father, and a wandering life began—a small house in Kensington for part of the year, winters in France and Switzerland, and summers with the grandmother in the old Scotch town that had sheltered Mary Stuart.

With the wanderings and wider view of the world came a glimpse of the world-embracing Faith—Christ's Church—a good deal of reading, many questionings, an interview with an Oratorian Father, and, finally, reception into the Church.

This was followed by attempts at writing, a sketch of "Devorguilla of Galloway," and her "Abbey of Dulce Cor," and a kindly letter from the saintly Father Dignam, S.J., then editor of *The English Messenger*. Then came encouragement from Father Matthew Russell; and a longer story in *The Month*, then in Father Clarke's hands; afterwards stories for Mr. Wilfrid Meynell in *Merry England*, in *The Catholic Magazine*, *The Fireside*, and one tale for the American *Messenger*.

Miss Packe.

BY FRANCES M. MAITLAND.

People were not astonished when Cecy Bathurst's engagement to Lord Lowdham was announced. That the Bathurst girls made good marriages had come to be recognized ; not that they were prettier, nor wittier, nor, if it came to that, better dowered than other girls, but " it was a way they had," to quote Mrs. Price, the rector's wife.

Had not old Mrs. Fawkes, of the Court, said, with decision, the moment she heard her nephew was on his way home from his Rocky Mountain expedition, " He will just be in time for Cecy ! "

Had not Colonel Falkiner, who had no respect for persons, poked his brother-in-law, the Rector, in the ribs, and whispered, " Another job for his Reverence, eh, Price ? " the very first time he saw the couple canter together up the street.

Had not poor Mrs. Bathurst herself said, with despairing presentiment, to her confidant, Miss Packe, "Oh, I hope Lowdham won't take a fancy to Cecy ! " A confidence responded to by a shake of the head that plainly said, " *That*, dear Mrs. Bathurst, no one can undertake to tell ! "

Mrs. Bathurst's worst enemies could not have accused her of being a match-making mother; her daughters' engagements invariably took her by surprise, and cost her many tears.

A young-looking woman still, gentle, patient Mrs. Bathurst lay on her invalid couch in the little morning-room all day. Her malady might, in the beginning, have been the vague disease hinted at by a strong-minded neighbor now and then—nerves, imagination, habit perhaps; but to the invalid herself the sufferings were very real, and Miss Packe, when catechized, had the mysterious "Ah, poor dear!" that impressed the listener more than a longer tale.

Little Dr. Bramwell, indeed, had been reported to have said that, if it had not been for Miss Packe encouraging her in her nonsense, Mrs. Bathurst would have been up and walking long ago; but even he had given up trying to rouse her, though he paid her a duty visit now and then.

Miss Packe, the "Dear Packie" of two generations of Bathursts, kept house, poured out tea, read history with Cecy, copied Mr. Bathurst's letters to *The Field*, nursed and spoiled Mrs. Bathurst, and was "worked to death among them all," according to Mrs. Price. Not that Packie thought herself ill-used; she confessed herself, to her friends, the happiest of women.

When there was not company, Mr. Bathurst took her to dinner "as if she had been the Queen;"

and if the house was full and she elected, as she often did, to sup in her school-room at dinner-time, Griffiths, the old butler, was sure to appear with a glass of port " with the master's compliments," and never failed to add the maccaroon he knew she loved, with an apologetic, " I thought you might like a biscuit, Miss."

Mrs. Bathurst had always a good-night kiss ready, a grateful pressure of the hand, and often a " What should we do without you, Packie, dear ? " that brought tears to the little woman's eyes.

Yes, Packie was happy, there was no doubt of that. She had been a pretty girl in her youth, and was a dainty-looking woman now, with bright brown eyes and rosy cheeks and snow-white hair, and had " kept her figure wonderfully," as the saying is. She had the " look " of the Bathursts that made Mrs. Price hint that she *might* be a poor relation after all; but it was the likeness that grows with long and loving intercourse, an accent, a mannerism, an expression sometimes.

A loyal, loving, faithful little woman, it was little wonder the Bathursts loved Miss Packe.

Time had stood still at Bathurst-Coombe, Lord Lowdham thought, when, the day after his arrival home, he followed Griffiths into the morning-room.

Mrs. Bathurst, the pale pink (conversation always brought) on her cheeks, was listening to Father Every, the chaplain, and the Rector, who were having an argument. Dante of course! Lowdham recognized the mellow Roman binding of the volume in the chaplain's hand at a glance.

Miss Packe in black silk gown, little silver caddy in hand, was anxiously watching her tea-kettle as of old; the Squire, in leggings, was leaning back in his big chair with Fix, the fox-terrier, on his knee, while Mary—they had not told him Mary Leake was at home—was perched on an arm of the chair, in a cool gray spring frock. How fresh and bright Mary always looked! Why, if Leake hadn't spoken so soon, who knew what might have happened! Lord Lowdham gave a little sigh. He had taken it all in at a glance as Griffiths announced him.

"Lord Lowdham." The Squire jumped up, Miss Packe put her caddy down; there were greetings, exclamations; he had had his hand nearly wrung off by the men, had been patted and rejoiced over by Mrs. Bathurst, and been shyly welcomed by Miss Packe, before he saw that the slim figure standing by her father's chair was not Lady Leake after all.

"What, you don't remember Cecy?" the Squire said, with a chuckle.

Time had not stood still after all; five years ago he had brought Cecy Bathurst—a doll!

"She is like Mary," Mrs. Bathurst said in her gentle way, while Cecy stood blushing under the general scrutiny.

Yes, Cecy was like her eldest sister, Lord Lowdham told himself, as he sipped his cup of tea—like Mary, but with a difference; taller, he thought, the teeth better too—and the hair! Was it because the Bathursts had naturally curly hair that it looked so soft and bright, and not dry and frizzled up like the hair of half the other girls he knew? Yes, Cecy's hair was just like Mary's—Kitty Tollemache's was darker, Louie Heron's too. But there! there were no girls like the Bathursts anywhere—sweet and frank and natural, and not too learned, Miss Packe had to be thanked for that! And always well-dressed, and never (hateful word) *smart!*

"Of course it was love at first sight," as Mrs. Price said when, not a month after the first meeting, the engagement was announced. But Mrs. Price liked Cecy Bathurst, her "bark was waur than her bite," and she rejoiced in the girl's happiness in her heart.

"What was the good of having daughters, if they ran away and left you as soon as they were grown up?" Mrs. Bathurst asked despairingly.

"Most mothers would consider you lucky," Mrs. Price responded dryly.

"I suppose some one will be running away with Packie next!" with a sigh.

"Ah, there we may trust Providence will be kind," said the Rector's wife.

"There was no hurry," the Squire protested, when Lowdham urged Cecy to name the day.

And why should they wait? Lord Lowdham expostulated, not unmindful of the grouse. Let them be married, take the run to the continent Cecy wished, and have a week or two at home before going north.

"'Happy's the wooing that's not long a-doing,'" quoted Mrs. Price. "The genus 'Bathurst girl' once extinct, some other of the Exshire young ladies may have their chance!"

"The Bathursts and Lowdhams were *old* Catholics," Mrs. Price was careful to explain to all newcomers. "She had no patience," she would add, "with perverts like the Tollemaches, and Sir John Leake. 'Reverts'? Did *Punch* really call them re-verts? Then *Punch* was a fool!"

Lowdham got his own way, and June saw Cecy Bathurst, with Dolly Price as bridesmaid, a wife; and Mr. and Mrs. Bathurst and Miss Packe settled down again, as best they might in the big house left daughterless.

"Cecy kept us young," the Squire complained, rubbing his rheumatic leg.

Fix haunted Cecy's room, and growled when the housemaids tried to displace him from her bed.

Mrs. Bathurst consoled herself with the pages of descriptive happiness sent nearly every day from the Tyrol.

She was always cold nowadays, she told Miss

Packe one day, making her feel her hands. Cold in July! and in that sunny room with a fire. Packie was not satisfied.

"Circulation, nothing but circulation," the doctor, who happened to be busy, said, not disguising his temper.

"Ah, poor dear!" Miss Packe began.

"Yes, that's just it, 'poor dear,'" the little man interrupted impatiently. "'Poor dear!' indeed! It's just what I have told you, all your fault, Miss Packe, encouraging her"—he paused for a civil word—"in these indolent ways. It's too late now, perhaps, but she ought to have been turned off that sofa twenty years ago. You had the matter in your own hands." And the little man rubbed his hands to show he washed them of the whole affair.

"Oh, poor dear!" Miss Packe repeated, wiping her eyes, "indeed you don't understand."

"I understand well enough." And with a grunt the busy little man was gone.

"It was losing Miss Cecy made the mistress so 'dwiney,'" the servants agreed; "And *most* unnatural if it hadn't and her the apple of her eye," Flint the maid added, resenting what she was pleased to call Miss Packe's "fuss."

Pretty Kitty Tollemache, who, summoned by Miss Packe, drove over the grays that were the envy of the country-side, to see her mother, agreed with Flint, and suggested that Lady Leake's little son and heir should be sent for to cheer up his grandmother. Packie mustn't be nervous, she added, as she kissed the little woman good-by; but Packie only shook her head.

It was quite a consolation to Miss Packe when the Lowdhams turned up a week sooner than was expected, and she was able to pour out all her anxieties and fears; but the next day found Mrs. Bathurst so much better it almost seemed as if Flint had been right after all. " I told you, Miss," that worthy said triumphantly, " it was only a-missing Miss Cecy—her ladyship, as I should say, begging her pardon."

The next day was the same. Mrs. Bathurst enjoyed her luncheon, enjoyed Lowdham's account of their wanderings and even adventures in the Tyrol, admired the presents brought from Paris, was wheeled, Cecy dancing by her side, as far as the east lodge, enjoyed her chat with Mr. and Mrs. Price who came to dinner, and told Flint while she was being put to bed, she didn't know how it was but she felt quite young somehow.

Packie never forgot that July evening when, Flint gone, she slipped in as usual to say good-night.

" How happy Cecy was, and Lowdham, how good ! " the mother said, rejoicing; then " Kiss me, Packie, I am tired."

" Not cold ? "

" No, not cold. Well, a little perhaps, but

nothing to worry about." But Packie, unsatisfied, wrapped her up.

She had said a second good-night and reached the door when Mrs. Bathurst spoke again. "You wouldn't leave Dick, would you, Packie?"

"Dick" was Mr. Bathurst; and while Packie, startled, paused for an answer, Mrs. Bathurst spoke again. "Good-night, Packie, I am going to sleep."

Packie was a good sleeper herself, owing, perhaps, to what may be called her perennial youth. Mr. Bathurst had a joke, called up on occasion, that made the little lady blush, that it took the fire-engine to wake Packie up. A story so far true, that when fire broke out in the schoolroom one early morning, the garden lads in their over zeal, had played the hose into the first open window they found, and soused poor Packie in her bed. But it scarcely needed Flint's trembling touch to rouse her on the sad July day that followed Cecy's coming home. Mrs. Bathurst had had a paralytic stroke.

Doctors and nurses came, in succession, from town. Daughters, hastily summoned, arrived.

Cecy, like a little ghost, haunted her mother's room, insisting she knew her, that she had moved her eyes, her hand.

The Squire refused to leave his wife's side. Father Every and the doctor, keeping vigil in the library, came up-stairs from time to time, joining their entreaties to Packie's that the Squire should take some rest; but the old man, older than his dying wife by twenty years, only shook his head; and in the early morning, her helpless hand tight locked in his, Mrs. Bathurst died.

That "Packie" was to look after Mr. Bathurst settled itself into the natural thing. Lady Leake, indeed, tutored by her husband that, as eldest daughter, she should, before leaving, make some arrangements for her father's comfort, began a little speech one day, only to break down in the first sentence and to throw her arms round Packie's neck with a sob and a "Oh, Packie dear! you know better than any of us what he likes," and "Indeed, I will do my best," Packie said, sobbing too.

The Squire took his sorrow simply and manfully, only begging that nothing should be meddled with or changed. So Mrs. Bathurst's great white couch and invalid table covered with books were left in their corner of the sunny morning-room, and the gardener brought, as of old, her favorite pots of flowers, and when the 20th of August came and Lord Lowdham, who had manfully resisted the grouse, could not resist the black game, Cecy and he went north, and the Squire and Miss Packe settled down to their new life. Packie doing the housekeeping, arranging the flowers, writing her orders as of old.

Sometimes the old man forgot his loss, and burst

into the morning-room where Packie, her work done, sat with her knitting, with a " Caroline, what do you think, a bearded tit was seen on the Denne Marsh yesterday!" or, " Caroline, what do you think, the beam-birds on the south wall are bringing out their second brood." And when the silence and empty sofa reminded him his wife was gone he would give a " Tut, tut," or " Dear, dear," and walk away; and Miss Packe would not see him again for an hour or two.

He liked to refer to his wife: " as Caroline, poor dear, would have said," or, " Caroline, poor dear, would have liked this or that," or he would remind Miss Packe of the days of their early married life, when " Caroline, poor dear, had been the prettiest girl in Exshire."

" Yes, Mary and Cecy were both like their mother. Kitty too, but they couldn't hold a candle to her." Miss Packe would bear him out.

The months went on; December came. " What? Not have the poor girls at Christmas! Tut, tut, that would never do. What would poor dear Caroline say to such a thing? Tut, tut! tut, tut! What was she thinking about? No, no, they must all come, all come. Yes, babies and all; yes, babies and all. Miss Packe must mind that—just as usual."

Perhaps the Squire found his first real consolation in Lady Leake's little three-year-old boy, who, if backward in speech, hugged the pointers and rushed to horses' heels in a way that enchanted his grandfather—if it drove his attendants distracted!

"A regular Bathurst, every inch of him," the Squire proclaimed with pride, when, lost one morning, he was found cuddled up in Brough's (the great mastiff) kennel in the yard. "If poor Caroline only could have seen him!"

Some of Packie's smiles, too, came back with the young folk. They had their Christmas presents for her, a miniature of Mrs. Bathurst—a joint gift—books, texts, what not! Even Freddy Tollemache had his present, given before dinner in the drawing-room, a brooch to fasten Packie's shawl, a silver pack of hounds in cry.

"Said to Kit the moment I spotted it, 'That's my present, Kit.' A *pack* of hounds! Good, isn't it? Ha, ha!"

And while Packie, with all her gratitude, looked at it askance, Kit said severely, "No one but yourself would see any point in such a foolish joke, Freddy!"

"It has its point, though! Come, Miss Kitty, confess," Freddy cried, seizing his wife's white arm.

"You are hurting me, Freddy, be quiet"—and Kitty pointed over the little red mark. "You ought to behave properly, it isn't"—and poor Kitty gave a sob—"it isn't like other years."

"If you mean I don't miss your poor mother, you're wrong," Freddy said with decision, "but she wouldn't grudge us a little joke, would she, Miss Packe?"

After all, Christmas went off "better than could have been expected," as Mrs. Price said, and indeed that lady did her best to help things along.

It was Freddy Tollemache, however, who specially took in hand the cheering up of the Squire, inventing, Kitty sadly feared, tales of shovellers that had been shot, and wild geese that had been seen on the Denne Lake. He even managed to secure a snipe with some peculiarity in its plumage that kept the Squire happy and excited for many a day.

"Packie had the patience of the saints," Freddy confided to his wife, when he saw the little woman putting the scraps of paper, quarter sheets, out of backs of envelopes, a sheet out of an old account-book perhaps, into order before copying out the Squire's communication to *The Field*, and putting away the volume after volume he had pulled down in verifying his facts, if facts, with Freddy's snipe's tale in question, they might be called!

After the Christmas gathering, life went on more cheerfully at Bathurst-Coombe. Little Dick Leake was left, with his nurses, for a time. Then spring came, and the home-farm, recently taken into his own hands, and talks with the bailiff, kept the Squire busy, and left little time to fret.

If poor Packie had her troubles with the household, she did not complain.

It had been all very well for the governess to have mistressed over them—as deputy, one might say—while the mistress was alive; but that, now she was dead and gone, Miss Packe was to have it all her own way, was "more than flesh and blood could stand, and enough to make Mrs. Bathurst turn in her grave," according to Flint, whom the Squire had refused to send away. "She had been a good maid to poor Caroline, and women always seemed to find sewing to do about a house!"

It was Freddy Tollemache who, coming in wet by the side-door one day he had ridden over to see his father-in-law, heard Flint "slanging" Miss Packe in the linen-room and went straight to the Squire; and, Flint pensioned off, and Griffiths solemnly bound over to report any further insolence, Packie was at peace.

It was on the anniversary of her mother's death that Cecy Lowdham's little daughter came. Mr. Bathurst walked over daily to inspect the little pink morsel of humanity that, lying in the portly nurse's arms, puckered up its face and doubled its fists, and did all a well-dispositioned baby should.

"No look of its poor grandmother," the Squire would say disconsolately, touching its cheek gingerly with a gentle finger-tip.

"And it was early days yet to say who her little ladyship would be like," Mrs. Naylor would cheerfully reply, with a dip in acknowledgment of the sovereign that so often found its way to her palm.

In Packie's opinion the baby had Mrs. Bathurst's eyes.

"I believe them when I see them," Freddy, who had made his way to the nursery, said. "Miss Packe, do you believe you were ever such a monster as that? A lobster's a joke to it!"

A monster indeed! Packie nearly cried. However, even Freddy was interested in hearing that it was a monster in another sense, had turned the scale at twelve pounds, according to Dr. Bramwell.

"Why, Kit's poor little beggar only weighed three and a half," Freddy cried; for Kitty had lost her only child.

Dr. Bramwell on his way home from Lowdham used to stop at Bathurst-Coombe to give Packie the last news of Cecy.

"Nothing wrong with Miss Packe?" the Squire asked anxiously one day, waylaying the little man in the hall.

"There is nothing wrong with Miss Packe," the doctor was happy to say.

"That was all right," the Squire, relieved, said.

Miss Packe in his opinion, the doctor rather stiffly went on, was an exceptionally healthy woman for her years—ex-ception-ally healthy, he repeated, rubbing his hands. Might he add that he had a great respect, he might say the greatest re-spect, for Miss Packe.

"Yes, yes, certainly." What on earth was the fellow driving at? the Squire asked himself.

If the Squire were not busy, Dr. Bramwell would be glad of a few words.

No, the Squire was not busy; he was at the doctor's service; but he thought ruefully of the bailiff setting out without him to the new cottages.

"The day was warm, what would the doctor have? A B. and S.?"

The day was certainly warm, to judge from Dr. Bramwell's appearance, as he sat mopping his forehead with a red silk handkerchief, in one of the big library chairs.

The brandy and soda, administered by Griffiths, perhaps gave him courage, for, thrusting the handkerchief into his pocket, and clearing his throat, he spoke.

"As I said, Mr. Bathurst, I have a great respect, a ve-ry great re-spect, for Miss Packe."

What on earth was the fellow after? the Squire asked himself again. Audibly—"He hoped they all had that."

"In fact,"—the doctor took another gulp from his glass and drew out the handkerchief again—"in fact, I have thought of it for some time. In fact—I have asked Miss Packe to be my wife."

The murder was out! "The——!" A bad word very nearly came from Mr. Bathurst's mouth; he walked to the window, walked back again, then back to the window, then turned. "She has accepted you?" Looking at little, red-faced, podgy Dr. Bramwell, Mr. Bathurst thought it unlikely!

"Well, *that* he could hardly say—Miss Packe had been—the Squire would understand—taken a lit-tle, yes, a lit-tle by surprise. Ladies always were, he believed, on these occasions. He! he!"

The little snob! The Squire felt inclined to kick him. "Surely, you know whether she said yes or no?" he demanded irately.

"Of course, of course." The little man was mopping his brow again. "That was just it. Miss Packe had been taken, as he had said, a lit-tle by surprise. It had struck him that Mr. Bathurst, perhaps, would say a word for him? He had a fair practice, had his savings, he could make her comfortable, he hoped."

"She is not young." The Squire spoke abruptly, he was provoked, angry—Bramwell want to marry *Miss Packe!* Advise Packie, who was as good as any of them—why, if her father hadn't got into that mess, Packie would never have been teaching at Bathurst-Coombe—advise her to marry little Bramwell, whose father had been the county vet! An honest little chap, no doubt,—but *Miss Packe!* The Squire fumed.

"He himself was fifty; *age*, if he might say so, had nothing to do with the *affection*. Yes, af-fection, if he might use the word, he had for Miss Packe." The little man spoke with some dignity.

He saw Mr. Bathurst was ruffled; naturally (he said to himself) he would not care to lose Miss Packe, who suited him to the ground, but it would be easy for the Squire, with his means, to find another housekeeper, or he might take the Herons to live with him, as many people thought he should have done when Mrs. Bathurst died; the Herons were hard up, as everybody knew.

"Look here, Bramwell"—the Squire, who had been walking up and down again, paused—"I never interfere in these matters. If a woman likes a man, she finds it easy enough to tell him so! If she doesn't—well. I'm not the man to persuade her to marry him against her will!"

"Ye-e-s," the little doctor spoke disappointedly; then more cheerfully, taking up his hat, "you'll at least wish me good-luck?"

"Good-luck? Of course I'll wish you good-luck," the Squire said testily, as he shook the departing visitor's hand.

Mr. Bathurst looked curiously at Miss Packe when they met at the luncheon-table. Her eyes and nose were red, her face flushed, her manner a little agitated. A first offer at fifty-six might naturally agitate, one may allow.

There was no doubt Miss Packe had been taken by surprise, she had been touched by Dr. Bramwell's devotion to Cecy, by his kindness in bringing her the daily bulletins—but that he should ask her to be his wife! After the little man's departure she had been as near hysterics as she had ever been in her life.

All the doctor had gathered, incoherently enough at the time, was, that it was impossible, quite impossible; and, when he had begged her to consider, she had sobbed " Yes, yes," only anxious to get him off.

The luncheon was a silent one, the Squire taking furtive glances at Packie now and then, regarding her in a new light, as a marriageable lady. Well, Bramwell was no fool; she was a fresh, sensible, comfortable-looking little woman, any man might be proud to call his wife.

Poor Packie, crumbling her bread, and vainly trying to swallow her roast mutton, was painfully aware of her flushed cheeks and swollen eyes.

" A glass of wine, Miss Packe," the Squire said presently, in, what he could not prevent from being, commiserating tones—" Griffiths, the wine to Miss Packe. Tut, tut, it will do you good ; Griffiths, fill up the glass. There, that's right, drink it up."

" Was she going to Lowdham that afternoon ? " he asked presently, when Griffiths, who also had been eying Miss Packe solemnly, had left the room.

" Not unless Mr. Bathurst had a message ; she had a letter—letter to write," Packie answered with some confusion, ready to cry again.

He was going himself, the Squire said ; then— " Look here, Miss Packe, as long as I am alive, and you are happy with us, your home's here. You understand."

And Miss Packe understood that the Squire knew all about Dr. Bramwell's offer, and grew scarlet.

Dr. Bramwell certainly did not speak of his own discomfiture, nor did Miss Packe, honorable little woman, tell tales; but in a few days every one, including Mrs. Price, knew that the little man had proposed and been refused.

If the Squire did tell Freddy Tollemache, it was in confidence, and if Freddy, through Mary Leake, who, as eldest matron of the Bathurst girls, was in charge at Lowdham, did send Cecy a pencil sketch of the Doctor on his knees offering Miss Packe a large heart. Cecy had hidden it under her pillow at once that the nurses might not see it and talk.

"The pair of them had more sense in their heads than she would have credited them with," Mrs. Price summed up. "Miss Packe would have made a most excellent wife, and Dr. Bramwell a—well, a detestable husband!"

"My dear! my dear!" charitable old Mr. Price said.

"By Jove, Kit, I believe Packie's got another sweetheart," Freddy Tollemache announced one day when he had come back from Bathurst-Coombe, about the end of November.

Litigation is not agreeable, but Mr. Bathurst's quick temper got him into many a scrape, and "before he knew what he was about," as he told Freddy, he had found himself deep in a complicated lawsuit with the outgoing tenant of the Home Farm.

"Compromise," Freddy advised. "It'll cost you a lot more than a few dirty bags of lime."

"It isn't the lime, it's the *principle*," the Squire said.

"Oh, hang the principle!" Freddy said. "Do the cheap thing these hard times." But the Squire would not be advised, and Mr. Omerod, senior member of the firm of Omerod, Green & Omerod, the Squire's London solicitors, was in constant requisition at Bathurst-Coombe.

"Fancy having an expensive fellow like that down, when old Wickham would have done just as well," Freddy said. "A nice bill your father will have! Omerod don't come for nothing, I can tell you that."

Freddy, an idle man, living with his father and mother, rode over to Bathurst-Coombe "to look the Squire up" nearly every day and brought Kitty back the news.

"You should see the eyes old Omerod makes at Miss Packe," he reported pretty regularly to his wife at this time.

"Don't talk nonsense, Freddy."

"Well, you'll see, Mrs. Kit! Look here, what will you bet?"

Even the Squire began to wonder—important

as, in his opinion, the case " Jones *versus* Bathurst" was—at the frequency of Mr. Omerod's Saturday to Monday visits.

Mr. Omerod, to be sure, was careful to explain on most of these occasions that he had only run down to have a friendly little talk over matters; and, to do him justice, none of the long confabs held in the smoking-room ever swelled Omerod, Green & Omerod's account.

Mr. Omerod, who had not long lost the old mother who had kept his house, was a bald-headed, professional-looking little man, nearly as stout, if not as red in the face, as Miss Packe's suitor, Dr. Bramwell. Mr. Omerod was, however, a gentleman, belonged to one of the Squire's own clubs, liked his dinner and his glass of wine, and did not hesitate to condemn either if bad.

Packie and Mr. Omerod were old acquaintances, of course.

"Miss Packe was well?" Mr. Omerod had hoped as usual, the first time he had run down about "the Jones affair," as the Squire drove him up from the station.

"Yes, Miss Packe was well," the Squire said, giving the mare a flick; then confidentially, with a glance at the groom behind, "Bramwell wanted to carry her off."

"Indeed," the lawyer looked his surprise, and both men laughed, but Mr. Omerod regarded Miss Packe with more interest than usual when they met before dinner that night, and, as it happened, Packie was looking her best, in new silk gown—Lady Leake's last gift—and soft lace fichu.

Mr. Omerod didn't want a giddy, dressy girl, fond of theatres and balls perhaps, to be at the head of his house; still less did he want a "frump," a plain, middle-aged person, in dowdy frock, like the Miss Baker his married sister Mrs. Green was pleased to recommend as an excellent future Mrs. Omerod. He wanted a good-looking, intelligent woman, not fond of gayety, but accustomed to society, whom he might be proud to introduce to his friends. How did it happen he had never thought of Miss Packe before? Quite a distinguished-looking person, the lawyer thought, observing her critically; healthy, good-natured, an excellent housekeeper—the Bathurst-Coombe dinners proved that—of his own faith (and that was imperative), of good family too. Why, Sir Howard Packe, the V.C. man, was Miss Packe's cousin, and he had married Lord Easthampton's daughter not so very long ago. Mr. Omerod almost thought it would do.

More than once at dinner, Mr. Omerod looked at the lady approvingly. Few women would have detected, now, that little over-soupçon of mace, and that new savory, picked up from Lady Lowdham's French cook, showed she was observant and knew "what was what."

In the drawing-room, after dinner, while Miss

Packe gave him his cup of coffee, Mr. Omerod examined her critically again. Yes, Miss Packe would look well at the head of the table in Gloucester Place. *It would do.*

By bedtime, Mr. Omerod had complimented Packie on her whist—the Squire, who knew the lawyer liked a good rubber, looking his surprise—and even managed to give her fingers a gentle squeeze as he bade her an emphatic " Goodnight."

On his next visit, Mr. Omerod brought Packie a wonderful hamper of bonbons, bristling with pink satin bows; he had had a run to Paris on business, he explained, and knew, with a tender smile, " ladies liked such things."

Then came the present of a book all the world was talking about, and (the lawyer thought) might possibly not yet have reached Bathurst-Coombe.

Miss Packe accepted these gifts in all simplicity, and spoke of Mr. Omerod as a " thoughtful man."

" You'll lose Packie this time, and no mistake," Freddy said to his father-in-law, when coming in one afternoon they found the lawyer assisting Miss Packe in concocting a menu for a dinner-party next day.

" Riz de veau à la monarque.
Cailles à la Bellevue.
Relevés.
Chapons braisés.   Sauce verte."

Mr. Omerod, pencil in hand, was reading with unction, aloud.

"By Jove!" Freddy said, "I pity Miss Packe when she's Mrs. O., and I pity old O.'s cook."

"Tut, tut," the Squire said, but he was genuinely put out. Could there be any foundation for what Freddy suspected? Omerod, certainly, had been very attentive to Miss Packe, now it was put into his head. But Miss Packe, at her age, never would be such a fool! And there had been Dr. Bramwell! "Tut, tut, tut, tut." The Squire went upstairs in quite a temper to dress.

"I suppose you will have the wedding here?" Mrs. Price said next evening to the Squire behind her fan, indicating Mr. Omerod and Miss Packe with a little nod.

"Wedding! what wedding?" the Squire's voice might have been heard all over the room. "There's no one going to be married here, so far as I know. You don't expect me to marry, I suppose? and Miss Packe ain't likely to change her state"—with a furious glance at Mr. Omerod, who, spruce, always gay, a white camellia in his button-hole, was bending over Miss Packe's teatray.

Freddy reported to his Kit that, impassioned as the old fellow might seem, there was no romance about his conversation, and mimicked his "and, my dear Miss Packe, I may without hesitation say, it was the best 'tortue claire' I ever tasted in my life."

Miss Packe was rather oppressed by the lawyer's

attentions. "He is much too fond of his dinner, my dear," she confided to Cecy Lowdham, which was a severe speech for gentle Miss Packe.

"Jones *versus* Bathurst" dragged along. Mr. Omerod went and came. Freddy, reporting progress to his Kitty (not just then allowed to drive), was confident of his bet.

At last a fatal morning came when Mr. Omerod, after a prolonged interview with Miss Packe in the morning-room, announced that he had business that must take him by the next train up to town; and when next instructions were wanted in the "Jones *versus* Bathurst" case, young Mr. Green came down to interview the Squire, and mentioned, incidentally, that just then the senior partner was much engaged.

A little flush used to come to Packie's cheek when Freddy Tollemache asked her if anything had been heard lately of Omerod, adding gravely that he had heard on good authority he was suffering from heart-complaint.

It became quite a little joke among the sisters to speak of Packie as a "dangerous little woman." "My dear, my dear," Packie would expostulate, blushing up to the roots of her hair.

The Squire recovered his serenity when he found he was not to lose Miss Packe. "Poor Caroline was right; she always said she was a sensible woman," he said to Freddy, who only hemmed.

But the Squire's peace of mind was not to be of

long duration. One morning a letter was handed to Miss Packe that caused that lady some agitation.

"Nothing wrong?" the Squire hoped, looking up from his newly opened *Times*.

"No, nothing wrong. Would Mr. Bathurst read for himself?" Miss Packe, half-laughing, half-crying, handed him the letter with trembling hand.

Mr. Bathurst looked rather grimly at the "Louisvale, Queensland," and the "Dearest Catharine" that began the letter, and turned with his more severe expression to the signature, "Your affectionate brother, John Packe." "Brother!" the Squire almost said his grace in his gratitude. Sweethearts had been getting so common with Packie, he had not known what to expect! John Packe; he remembered, the brother that had not been heard of for years. Well, for Packie's sake he was glad he had written at last. He was not so glad as he read on. John Packe regretted—on the thinnest of paper, and in the faintest of inks—that he had kept his sister so long in ignorance of his whereabouts. People got careless at these up-country stations somehow, and time flew faster than one realized, and Cathy must forgive him, as the writer knew she would. Times had been bad, too, as Packie must have seen, if she read the newspapers, which the writer supposed she did. In John's opinion matters were going from bad to worse, and, having his opportunity, he had sold his station, and was coming home, if not a rich man, a *warm* one, even for the old country, and Packie could say good-by to her teaching and look forward to a comfortable home.

"O Jack, Jack!" Packie—to the Squire's dismay—was crying. Was she glad to leave them, then?

"He had taken his passage in the *Morning Star* and would be home nearly as soon as the letter." The Squire had nearly missed this postscript.

The *Morning Star*—the Squire had seen the name that very day—he turned to his *Times;* yes, here it was: she had made one of the quickest passages known, had nearly broken the record in fact.

"O Jackie, Jackie!" Miss Packe was sobbing still. Griffiths had discreetly left the room.

"We must expect to lose you, I suppose?" the Squire spoke gruffly.

"Oh, indeed, indeed!" Packie sobbed, she could say no more.

Had the whole world combined against him? the Squire asked himself. Bramwell, Omerod, and now this ne'er-do-well brother—who nevertheless had made his pile—from the end of the world! The Squire would not, to do him justice, have grudged Packie any happiness, but Bathurst-Coombe without her after all these years! Quite vividly the Squire saw his solitary meals, his library table littered with the scraps which only Packie had patience to put straight and copy (he did not himself pretend to be able to read the hieroglyphics put down in haste). Then Caroline had been so fond of Miss Packe! Poor Caroline! And Miss Packe had been so devoted to her.

There seemed to the Squire only one way to get out of the difficulty. The resolution was made in haste, as the Squire's resolutions always were. He walked round the table and laid a not ungentle hand on Miss Packe's shoulder, "Look here, Miss Packe, be my wife."

Was the sky falling! Miss Packe got up. Stay as Mr. Bathurst's wife! Take Mrs. Bathurst's place! What could the Squire think of her to suggest such a thing? With one reproachful glance, Miss Packe fled the room.

" But what is it all about, father ? " Mary Leake, who was staying at Lowdham and had been driven over by Cecy that afternoon, asked.

She had found her father sitting disconsolately in the library; she had left Packie in tears, with Cecy, up-stairs.

The Squire, fidgeting in his chair, made no response.

" She may be sorry to leave us (dear Packie, not half so sorry to leave us as we shall be to lose her), but I cannot see why her brother's home-coming should upset her so."

" Nor I, my dear," the Squire said, seeing she was waiting for an answer. And then—he was an honest man, and Mary and he were bosom friends —" The truth is "—the Squire cleared his throat— "tut, tut! tut, tut." He paused again, looked hard at his daughter, and went desperately on—" I asked her to be my wife!"

"Father!" Mary Leake sat for a moment dismayed, then the ludicrous side of the affair struck her, and she began to laugh. "Father, poor father!" she said when she could speak, patting him on the knee. "And Packie, poor Packie!" She began to laugh again.

The Squire sat shame-faced. "Well, my dear, it no doubt strikes you as absurd, but I didn't know what I should do without her, you see."

"Yes, I see." Mary began to laugh again; then, more gravely, "Look here, father dear, leave it all to me, you don't want to marry Packie, and Packie doesn't want to marry you; it's all that wretched brother, and I'll tell you what we must do—*marry him!* Men that come from the colonies all marry, I think. Have him down, and we'll see what we can do."

"Mary," the Squire said, quite relieved by this unburdening of himself, "you remind me of your poor mother. Poor Caroline!"

It really was providential, as Mrs. Price observed (for what could the Squire have done without Miss Packe?) that John Packe should have found his fate, as so many men have done before him on board ship on his passage home, not that that was

to make any difference, he assured his sister; his
Ellen was looking forward to her making her home
with them.

"I told you so, father," Mary Leake said triumphantly, when she heard the news. She and
her husband and babies had come over from Lowdham that there might be no "awkwardness" for
Packie.

Whatever happened, Freddy was not to be told,
Cecy and Mary had agreed; and Mary had added
in a guilty whisper, "Cecy, I often think Freddy is
a little—well, coarse, you know!"

Poor Mary had some difficulty in making it up
between Packie and her father—"that he should
have thought I would do such a thing," the poor
lady always repeated among her tears—but at last
peace was made. She took Father Every into her
confidence, and the priest, not without a twinkle in
his eye, gravely assured Packie it was her *duty*
(with emphasis) to stay at Bathurst-Coombe; and
after a solemn shaking of hands and a "Tut, tut!
Miss Packe, you shouldn't have been so hard on an
old man" from the Squire, the pair settled happily
down, "till death should them part"—according
to Freddy. (How *did* Freddy always know everything?)

"Packie, you dangerous little woman!" Mary
Leake often said.

"My dear, it was never my fault," Packie would
humbly protest.

MRS. WILLIAM MAUDE.

MRS. WILLIAM MAUDE (née Sophie Dora Spicer) was brought up in one of the loveliest of English deer-parks, her parents going to live there when she was ten years old, and there she wrote her first stories in nursery and schoolroom days, but these never appeared in print.

Her first publication was a little story written in aid of the Sick Children's Hospital in Great Ormond Street. It was brought out by the S. P. C. K., and called " Cyril's Hobby-Horse." The proceeds went to the Children's Hospital.

About the same time (when twelve years old) she ventured to send a story to *Aunt Judy's Magazine*, which was declined, but "Aunt Judy's" letter was religiously treasured; a kind, sympathetic letter, beautifully worded as only Mrs. Gatty knew how to write.

"Two little Hearts" was her next publication.

Mrs. Maude was never sent to school, but shared her younger sisters' masters in their Belgrave Square schoolroom during successive London seasons, while the elders went to balls and parties.

After a few years she was received into the Catholic Church, and lived some time abroad. She gave up writing for a while, but soon began again, and through Monsignor Nugent, then editor of *The Fireside*, her stories appeared from time to time in both the *Catholic Times* and *Catholic Fireside*. The Catholic Truth Society has reprinted one of these, "The Runaway Marriage," and is now bringing out a little volume of her short stories.

In 1890 she became Mrs. William Maude. Her husband belongs to the old Yorkshire family of Maude; he is a barrister, and she thinks he should be called "the children's friend," his interest in the spiritual welfare of Catholic workhouse infants being so well known.

Mrs. Maude's book, "The Child Countess," appeared in 1893, and she has another almost ready which will, perhaps, lead to greater thought and realization of that spirit world so close to us and to which we are all hastening, the purgatory where each suffering soul awaits its deliverance from pain. Its present title is "A Prisoner of Purgatory," but it is not certain whether it will be published under that name.

A Paste Buckle.

BY SOPHIE MAUDE.

I.

> "Be merry," he said, " sweetheart, to-day,
>   While the merry birds do sing!
> Next month will be the month of May,
>   And the trees are blossoming;
> And well I wot, by God His grace
> We have looked this hour," he said, "on the face
>   Of one that shall be King!"
>
> —MAY PROBYN.

SOME time during the last century when men went bravely apparelled as their fathers did before them, vying with fair women in silks and laces, the shoe-buckle belonged to a young prince. You smile, while you ask, Is it a fairy story? No, though his court was something of a fairy's creation, lasting a night and a day. The lines of life are so interwoven and twisted together that, strangely enough, the prince's paste buckle has to do with a long-forgotten love-tale in which he played no part, and there it lies hidden away among the brown rose-leaves and dead lavender stalks of a century.

* * * * *

Just so long ago as our great-*great*-grandmothers' days, a boy went singing up and down near a beautiful fountain, where pigeons were sunning their purple breasts by the rushing water. His sweet voice mingled with the roar and splash of great cascades in the pathetic strains of Palestrina's music. He was learning part of the Mass called after Pope Marcellus, and stood still now and again to repeat a bar or two, beating the air with uplifted hand to mark the time. The pigeons were the only audience in this street rehearsal. It was just midday. A few women came drowsily along. Men were sleeping on the street-corners, there was a clanging of bells overhead. They seemed ever so slightly to stir the warm, scented air. The boy finished his song and turned away down the street, his long, scanty cassock throwing a sharp black shadow behind him. In the villa gardens over the wall the oranges and lemons hung themselves out like gold and silver balls. A new song, yet ever old, the birds sang to their mates, and the trees were just budding into blossom. The boy, too, went a-wooing. His love was a nut-brown maid, beautiful to look upon, with sparkling eyes and raven hair, and they wandered hand-in-hand through golden orange groves to the tune of the old, old song the birds kept singing. Overhead the tree-trunks were hidden by a growth of creeping glory, white and purple blossoms against the blue ethereal sky of Italy.

It was pleasant to look upon those two: to see the boy's fearless love, and the girl's soft glances where the warm red blushes came through her rich brown skin.

"I think the winter should never come," she murmured, slipping down among the grasses; "it would be sweet to have spring always, only spring!" She gave a little shiver, and just then a shadow came across the sun. Some one was approaching stealthily over the mossy turf, and a voice spoke before she was well aware of a strange presence there.

"*Bella mia*, permit me." A kiss upon her cheek, and a hand laid caressingly on her hair—a white hand flashing with rings. All the brightness vanished with the sound of her scream. The boy sprang to his feet while her frightened cry rang up among the trees. The face was hidden from her against the glaring sunlight, and the boy with all the strength of a young lion rushed upon the unknown, who, not prepared for this sudden charge, reeled backward into the arms of a young man following closely upon his heels.

"*Per Bacco!* 'tis an infant Hercules. Excuse me, signor, but to sip honey from so fair a flower is the pleasure, nay, the positive duty of every cavalier!"

But his companion dragged him back, expostulating. "Nay, let him be, Vitalio, you have worked the very mischief here; the lady is frightened—make apology for so ill a part!" The voice and its refined accents sounded pleasant enough, but the boy panted with rage, scowling angrily into eyes that met his own with the light of a good-humored smile.

"You appear amused, signor, but I am not. This lady is my affianced wife and you have offered her an insult!" The girl had risen to her feet and was clinging with a pretty gesture of confidence to her lover's side; he put his arm around her and felt proud in that moment to be her strong protector.

The slight boyish figure and shy dignity with which he stood brought another smile into the stranger's face—not a happy smile, neither was the face a pleasant one. His companion spoke in low musical speech:

"Who are you? Let me have your name, young sir," he said. The tone was one of authority, and it surprised and disconcerted the boy. He had much ado to set aside his blustering anger, while his sweetheart pulled his sleeve and whispered:

"Don't be angry, *amor mio!* Answer him nicely, he's a great gentleman and looks kind."

"I am Felice Morelli, one of the singers at Sant' Andrea delle Fratte," began the boy thus prompted.

"His voice is lovely," the girl broke in eagerly.

"I live at Palazzo Poli, and I—that is, *we*—are betrothed and to be married some day."

"*Bella voce?*" questioned the younger of the two men in his musical voice that in itself attracted the lad even if it had not been accompanied by a face of more than ordinary beauty. "I have it! I will make you one of our own musicians. Come to-morrow about noon to Palazzo Muta-Savorelli; you understand me, *caro mio?* And meantime consider yourself as engaged in our service. Will that make up for the stupid impertinence to your pretty *promessa sposa?*" A careless nod and wave of a jewelled hand, and then the two gentlemen had passed out of sight. The boy and girl were left standing alone.

"What eyes! What a face! *Maria santissima*, he is some one very great and grand!" exclaimed the nut-brown maid.

"Did you hear him? Palazzo Savorelli! My fortune is made." Then out of the very joy of their hearts those two took hands and began gambolling over the grass under the glorious blossoming creepers that swung above their heads in triumphal arches and scattered petals of bright gold under their dancing feet. It was only when they stopped to rest that the boy could find breath to say: "It is the Principe Carlo Edoardo, and he is a king's son!"

Here was wonderful news indeed, and the two bade each other good-by, Tita to return to her Aunt Beppa Elisabetta, Felice to run home to his mother at the Cardinal's Palace where they lodged. Felice was no prince though he lived under the same roof with a Cardinal of the Holy Roman Church, and though his mother Concetta wore real pearls in her great gold earrings fit for a princess!

II.

Not far from Sant' Andrea delle Fratte a great portico stands back, and into its yawning depths, out of the sunshine, plunged Felice. Up wide stairs, across a dim cloister of white statues and camellia-trees to a cool loggia at the top of the palace. There a queer shuttered window in a little room was hung with pale, tender-hued vine-leaves, framing as in a picture the grandest dome in the world. It was a picture that greeted his waking eyes, and it was the last they fell upon at night across the city's twinkling lamps. It was like music to his soul, and the boy loved it, the music of light and beauty. To-day his mother was waiting for him, and hastened to lay aside her spinning as his dark head appeared above the last step of the long stairs.

"There is news to-day, glorious news!" he cried, and over a bowl of savory mess Felice told the story of the prince, carefully omitting the courtier's rude insult to his fiancée. "You will be glad now, *madre mia!* You will let us soon be wedded? My fortune is made. I shall have a big salary and ever so many fine clothes."

"I looked to a better wife for my son than that little girl from Spoleto!" said Concetta.

And Felice answered as he had often answered before: "She is a rose among flowers; she is more beautiful than any other girl of them all when they come to draw water at the fountain. My Tita carries her head like a swan, and her white teeth, when she smiles, twinkle like stars! And did you ever see hair like hers? Black as night, with a bright tinge from the sun; and such arms, such a neck, and little fairy feet that trip so daintily over the stones. Ah, *madre mia*, you are hard to please indeed!"

"But have I not always said so? Do these make qualities for a wife? Have you asked if she can spin the quicker for all her beauty? or sew, or cook the best among them all? Do you know whether she is sweet or sour? or what *dota* she may bring her husband?"

"Sweet she is as any summer flower; and as to her portion, when I am singer up at the Palace yonder I shall earn enough and to spare for us both."

"You are too young, I tell you, to think of marriage; and as to Tita, a month ago she wasn't in Rome. I pray you what do you know of her?"

Concetta raised her hands and cast up her eyes to heaven, while her son repeated musingly: "A month ago—yes, just that time I have known her. She came from Spoleto to lodge with her Aunt Beppa Elisabetta, just a month ago!"

"*Pazienza*, bright eyes and white teeth don't go to make steady housewives——"

But Felice was out in the loggia by this time, putting an end to the conversation. Would his mother never consent to their union? In Italy marriage is not thought of without a parent's blessing. Felice was nineteen and Tita three years younger. The boy and girl were betrothed, but Concetta refused to give her consent further than this. He would fain have presented his bride with the ancient heirloom his mother wore upon her fat middle finger—a ring with a strange foreign inscription, with a miniature painting, and a beautiful pearl for constancy. It had been Concetta's own betrothal-ring, and was given her by that great northern lady, Felice's foreign grandmother. But Concetta stoutly refused it except to a daughter-in-law of her own choosing. "I will never give it you, or my blessing either. You espouse her over the dead body of your broken-hearted mother!" she would exclaim tragically. "There's Marietta, a good steady girl, and Gemma, my own godchild, and Assunta of the Trastèvere, and Maria of the Drogheria (where your poor father always went for his apothecary stuff), and Lucia——" But here the list of eligible partners would break off and the poor woman always burst into a violent fit of crying which her son vainly endeavored to assuage.

He had kept all his savings for the purchase of a betrothal-ring of cunning workmanship—two hearts transfixed by cupid's dart upon a blue enamelled ground—and now there was a prospect of riches in the future, it would be hard indeed if his mother did not give her consent. The prince had come to set all things straight like the fairy prince in a story-book! This was his thought as he stayed to draw water from the loggia. With what a noise and splash the bucket slipped into the well, and the boy's strong young arms pulling at the rope, up it came, scattering great sparkling drops as the sun caught and kissed the overflowing rim into a thousand diamond flashes. To Felice's happy eyes even the battered old bucket looked glorified then. And Felice's mother, like many another, was obliged to keep her forebodings to herself, since the young must learn by hard experience what they won't take second-hand from the old. And out in the mellow sunset, when the bells rang *Ave Maria*, the boy went on repeating his oft-told tale of love to the beautiful girl at the fountain-side.

A week more and Felice had become one of the king's musicians, his threadbare cassock was exchanged for the black velvet and silk stockings of the gentlemen choristers, and his hair curled u o a fine white ruff. "You only want a gold cha n said his mother, "to look the gentleman born indeed you are!" And she nodded her head my teriously towards the old oak chest where she ke the ring of British workmanship, the heirloom from his English grandmother.

III.

Oh, green is forsaken
And yellow's forsworn,
But blue is the prettiest color that's worn!
—Old Ballad.

Tita had played at love, had broken hearts before she was fifteen! When she left Tivoli to make her home with her aunt in Rome, it was with strict injunctions from her *madre* to Beppa that she would look carefully after Tita, and get her speedily married. Tita's aunt thought her duty done when she chose the son of her old friend Concetta Morelli—the son who inherited all his father's musical talent, and must some day rise above the common grade of peasant. But the girl had promised herself "a gentleman husband." The fatal day came when a pair of bold black eyes fascinated her, and when Felice came to her in his sorrow, "I am sent to England by the Prince's own desire!" a strange triumphant gleam shot from Tita's cat-like eyes. "My love," he said, "we must part! England is far away——" a sob rose in his voice.

"To England? You are sent to England?" Again the wild gleam in her eyes, but it died out immediately.

"*Amor mio*, I am sent to carry despatches from the English King to his own people. I have a buckle from the Prince's shoe—a pledge from His Highness to the great lord to whom I am sent. Yes, a poor musician is the best disguise for the safety of the papers; no warrior among them all can go so safely as your poor Felice!"

"But such a long journey!" she said feverishly, while her eyes glittered.

"Yes, and the expense is undertaken by our old enemy the wicked Marchese. But yes, is it not wonderful? I shall earn the King's favor, but I would sooner not have been beholden to the man who insulted you, *carina*! Do not turn away your head, my dove, my dear one; the parting will be over some day,—and then——"

His voice had a triumphal ring in it of the joy to come. Her shallow girl's heart felt at that instant the sharp stabs of remorse. "It is Our Lady's month, a happy omen. Will you wear a knot of blue ribbon for me, against my return?" asked the young lover with the ribbon in his hand. "Indeed I know you will be true to me." How could he doubt her, whose own nature was all truth and loyalty?

The girl answered grudgingly that blue became her ill, but she would "see about it." With that half promise Felice started on his journey.

Our Lady's month, Mass heard in the church he loved so well, and then Rome was behind him, and his heart beat quick. Is it not a marvellous thing, the first setting forth on a journey, when one is only nineteen and the long untried years still lie before one in the future's golden womb, mysterious and unknown?

The boy's first resting-place was hardly passed when a messenger overtook him. Felice recognized the livery of the Marchese's servants; and while he wondered, the messenger had thrust a packet into his hand, and immediately galloped off. All Tita's treachery was known to him when he broke the seal. She was to be married that morning to the evil man who had bewitched her, and she had chosen the time when Felice, bound by royal command, was powerless to go and save her! The boy flung himself on the ground in those first moments of agony. His fierce southern nature prompted him to call death to his aid in his despair, but something, he knew not what, restrained him in his mad desire. Was it the protection of the Sacred Heart, the presence of One unseen to whom Mary's children are specially dear?

There was one drop of comfort even now—a broken-hearted but very loving letter came to him from his mother. It was written by the public letter-writer on the piazza, and, wrapped in the thick parchment-sheet, lay the ring he had so often longed for, his grandmother's miniature set in English gold.

Felice felt he cared nothing for it now, but he tied it up carefully in its paper wrappings and placed it with the prince's paste buckle under his jacket, before he went on his journey. But the song he had set out with in the morning was hushed. His eyes were full of tears. The glory of the night was spread above him now, but he saw nothing of its beauty. The long vine-tendrils took hands across fields of blue flax and odoriferous clover. They seemed to dance airy dances above the flower-cups in the pale moonlight, the southern stars shone like globes of golden splendor, and the fireflies glittered, but he only saw them through a vale of tears. Yet in the years to come when Felice's youth was past, the man thanked God for the boy's crucible of pain!

IV.

The little god of love.
—NURSERY RHYME.

THE first day of October had come. Eldred Manor House with its shady lawns and high beech hedges, four centuries old, under the green Berkshire downs, looked cool and inviting in the hot afternoon. The harvest was late this year, but now the corn was all carried. All the village of Eldred had turned out to assist in the carrying. The Squire rode up the lane on his big cob and the neighbors had come to the harvest feast. It was all a familiar scene to English eyes. After the supper was over and the Squire's good cider had made even the least jovial merry, the fiddler was called for, and the tables were removed for a dance on the sward, but there was a cry of consternation when the news went round that the musician had cut his hand and could not play. One or two of those present offered to supply his place, but they were received with dubious shakes of the head from those who knew the musical prowess of these volunteers. A disappointed silence succeeded the hum of voices at first eagerly raised, but the Squire, unwilling to be balked of his favorite pastime, led out the prettiest of his tenants from the crowd and, humming a snatch, kept time with his nail-studded boots to the girl's tripping feet upon the grass. Just at this moment, while a few rough voices, much out of time and tune, followed the gentleman's lead, the damsels timidly elbowing their chosen swains, the portly butler advanced and announced "a foreign gentleman who had brought his fiddle all the way from Italy, and would his worship be pleased to hear the lad play?"

"Mind the forks and spoons!" cautioned his worship in an audible aside. "Yes, Robbins, bring him in; we want music badly—music we must have at any price, since Dan the fiddler——" His further speech was cut short by the entrance of a pale young man, dark-eyed and dark-haired, in velvet coat and small-clothes frayed and worn, and powdered with white dust from the road,—a slender youth,—who bowed low to the company, and with hands that evidently trembled with exhaustion commenced to draw out a small violin from a shabby leathern case. Felice? Yes, it was Felice! White-lipped, haggard, tired out with his weary march through unfamiliar scenes and hard, rough ways—he had travelled most of the way on foot. He looked round on the strange English faces. Most of them met his weary gaze with a stolid bucolic stare. He had not broken his fast for twenty-four long hours, but Eldred was the village marked on his rough pocket-map, the nearest to Rackenford, whither he was bound with those precious letters, the despatches from King James III. If these good people would reward his fiddling with a few silver coins, he could pay his way to the castle, where his long journey would end at last. If only the mist before his eyes would clear, if only his hands would not shake so that he could hold his bow at the proper angle and play the dance-music required.

"Father"—would he ever forget the dear accents of that sweet voice? The tones of it must needs make music in the spheres—"Father, see, the young musician is faint, he must not play till he has broken his fast."

Through the mist that has somehow gathered in his poor tired eyes, Felice sees a tender girlish form, a fair face wreathed in golden hair, the eyes as blue as speedwells—ethereal china-blue that is so seldom seen, except perhaps in little children's eyes—what wonder if the young Italian take this fair English maiden for an angel, his guardian angel, come to succor him in his last hour?

A wall of great darkness is shutting him in, there is a sound like many waters in his ears, and, with no word of warning, he suddenly falls in a death-like faint upon the grass.

"Bless my soul!" ejaculates the Squire, "don't be frightened, Pen; don't be alarmed, dear heart; the heat has overcome him, but he is not dying,—no, nor near it. Bring some wine, Robbins, stand back, good people, so—he'll revive if you'll give him time."

But Felice does not revive though the simple people do all they know, and after awhile they lift up his prostrate form and carry him, still sleeping that sleep of death, across the grass and into the house. The long swoon lasts till the sunset is flooding the old dark walls with blood-tints and splashing all the white bed where he lies in a crimson lake. The boy starts up in horror, his eyes wide opened. He cries faintly, "Is it blood? Have they killed me? Are the letters safe?" He falls back shuddering, but a soft hand is laid on his arm, and gentle tones murmur words of rest and comfort. His fluttering eyelids close, and he falls asleep to dream of the angel with blue eyes and golden hair. When he wakes again the angel is by his side. She brings wine and food and raises him in her arms to drink, while a faint blush overspreads her fair face beneath his eyes fixed so earnestly upon her.

"I think I have been dreaming," he says; "pray, madam, tell me who you are and where I am." English is easy now to Felice.

"This is Eldred Manor House, and my father has ridden for help, but the physician is difficult to find and may be long a-coming. I am glad you can eat; it is better than medicine, sir."

"But what is your father's name, and who are you?" the lad asks with simple directness.

"My father is Squire Mornington, and I am his daughter Penelope. I have no mother; she died, sir, a long time back. Oh! we were very sorry to see you fall ill. Ah, but you are better!"

"Have I been ill? Yes, I remember now." He draws his hand, so slender and white, across his eyes. How fine the ruffles are at his wrists! Surely, she thinks, in spite of such worn attire, the young musician must be a gentleman! While she wonders about him, his thoughts are of her, and their eyes meeting—was it then?—a flash of sympathy like a chain of gold draws their hearts together. The girl's two hands are clasped upon her knee as she sits demurely at the window, a fairy thing with her wreath of yellow hair and eyes like blue forget-me-nots. She hastily averts them when they meet his own, and this is how Felice came to know Penelope—Penelope Mornington!

V.

> "Loyal je serai durant ma vie!"
> —Song.

The days that followed were the sunniest, and that particular October month was the brightest, that had ever dawned on this old wicked world of ours since it first began. Penelope could not have told you, she could not have analyzed her feelings, but she knew that she was happy—yes, happy as the day was long! True, the despatches had to be taken to their destination, and her new friend bade her farewell for at least three days, but what did that signify? Did not her father, at heart an ardent Jacobite, mount Felice on his own best horse, and allow Penelope to be of the party to Rackenford Castle?

Felice was received as a distinguished guest, the prince's ambassador, the honored messenger from "the king over the water."

The boy wore his laurels modestly. When opportunity served he told of his poverty and of the prince's kindness, and how he hoped some day to gain distinction in music.

The great man to whom he delivered his despatches, and with them his precious pledge, the Prince of Wales' buckle—the shoe-buckle that shone like diamonds, but that was only paste, for the diamonds had been pawned long ago—admired Felice's voice and offered a high price if the lad would accept the post of tenor among the singers at Rackenford Castle. His Majesty King James could ill afford to pay his musicians even the small salary allowed them; gold was more plentiful in an English castle than a Roman palace. But the boy, true to his allegiance, refused the tempting bribe. The county people, following the example of the great lord who patronized the stranger, engaged Felice to sing and play at their syllabub parties and fashionable entertainments. He gave music-lessons to the squires' wives and daughters. Haughty young madams fresh from town invited the handsome Italian to their country-houses.

The castle was Felice's home until he should earn sufficient to pay his journey back to Rome, but his happiest days were spent at the old house amid the Berkshire downs. During his hours of work or recreation his thoughts were with Penelope in the music-room at Eldred Manor. There was always one face he could not forget, one voice that—school his heart, control it as he would—set his pulses beating and made his eyes grow bright. When the young companions who came to share Mistress Mornington's lessons had returned home, the boy master and his pupil would sit and talk in the deep embrasure of the window or by the chimney-corner. When the Squire came in early from the hunting-field and saw them thus, he was glad to find his lonely child so well amused.

"Pen is a baby yet, in pinafores but yesterday," he told himself; "there is no danger!" and with that dismissed the subject.

Penelope could not hear too often, could not ask enough about the royal princes exiled for the faith. She saw the paste buckle when Felice handed it to the personage to whom it was sent, and had knelt in simple reverence to kiss the royal crown above the brilliant setting of the stones.

One day in the twilight he showed her his mother's ring. He had only regarded it carelessly in his dejection at Tita's treachery. Now he was startled to meet Penelope's blue eyes looking at him out of the miniature. "It might be your portrait, dear madam!" he exclaimed, "it is so like—so like!"

"And here is our name," cried the girl, and she read in the fading light, "P. Mornington." "How marvellous!" They could talk of nothing else. But when Penelope, in the innocence of her heart, desirous that her father should share her pleasure in this "new-found cousin," showed Felice's ring, the Squire spoke coldly of "poor relations" and muttered something about "a *mésalliance* in the past." Happily the young man did not hear, for the hot southern blood in his veins would not have borne the insult.

The time had come for his departure, and alas! they two were lovers. Felice's heart was in Penelope's keeping. Penelope's heart beat only for him. The golden hours had slipped away so quickly, Felice's birthdays had come and gone. He was twenty-one. She was just eighteen. Ah, love at eighteen! Penelope could not hide it, she would not have hidden it if she could. On the morning that her lover said farewell, she flung herself weeping into her father's arms and asked to cross seas with Felice as his wedded wife. Felice on his knees before the Squire with southern vehemence declared his willingness to wait, as Rachel's lover waited—to work seven years if need be for the lady of his heart. The sequel might have been expected, but it was none the less heartbreaking, when the Squire drove him from the room and from the house, swearing great oaths at the foreigner's impertinence, vowing to horsewhip the presumptuous stranger round the marketplace.

And amid the storm of bitter reproaches, Penelope's lover was forced to ride away sobbing—yes, his manhood was not ashamed by those tears—weeping because he must see his love no more.

Many months after, Felice knelt before the shrine of the apostles in great St. Peter's, as he had knelt with Penelope in the rustic chapel at Eldred—the old church that had never been desecrated by Protestant worship. The Morningtons were Catholics like their ancestors before them, and he could picture the girl he loved pouring out her heart in prayer for him. Felice's mother **was** dead. It was not long after this that the Squire of Eldred, outlawed and a beggar, his estates confiscated in the cause of King James III., fled for his life, and the lovers met once more. It was in Rome at the royal palace where the King lived. Felice had been appointed "Chapel Master;" the King had knighted him in honor of his successful mission to England.

Penelope Mornington and her true knight were happily married, and though the most disastrous page of modern history was unfolded before them, their own lot was a peaceful one. The Squire found comfort in waiting on his king in exile, and in lavishing all his affection on "Pen" and the husband he had once so cruelly insulted. Penelope's little daughter came as a messenger of peace to the exiled family.

After all, was not the prince like the good fairy in a story-book? His shoe-buckle brought great happiness into two young lives.

CLARA MULHOLLAND.

Miss Clara Mulholland is a daughter of the late Joseph Stevenson Mulholland, M.D., of Belfast, and younger sister of Miss Rosa Mulholland (Lady Gilbert). Miss Mulholland was born in Belfast, but left that town at a very early age. She was educated in Loughborough, Leicestershire, England, at a convent of the Sisters of Providence of the Institute of Charity, and afterwards at a convent of the Dames de Marie, Coloma, Belgium. Her first story, for young children, was published by Messrs. Marcus, Ward & Co., of Belfast, and by John Murphy, of Baltimore. Then followed " Naughty Miss Bunny," " The Strange Adventures of Little Snowdrop," and " Little Merry Face and His Crown of Content." Of late, Miss Mulholland has written stories for various London magazines and papers, and for Messrs. Tillotson & Sons, of Bolton, and the National Press Agency, London. Her other books are: " A Striking Contrast," " Kathleen Mavourneen," " The Miser of King's Court," " Percy's Revenge " and " Linda's Misfortunes."

Mave's Repentance.

BY CLARA MULHOLLAND.

She had always been the belle of the village. At patterns and fairs, at wakes and dances, Mave was the admiration of all. She was tall and strong for her eighteen years, with a neat, well-shaped head crowned with a coronet of nut-brown hair; a skin like the inside of a shell, so dainty its coloring; and eyes of the deepest blue, that looked black in the shadow of the long dark lashes.

Mave McMahon was the child of a poor fisherman in Innisboffin, a small island off the west coast of Ireland; and in these days of her golden youth worked in the fields, carried baskets of seawrack upon her head, or tended her father's sheep as they browsed upon the hill-side. Mave knew little of the great mainland that lay beyond the sea. Her whole world was in the island where she had been born, and she wished for nothing more. To live and die there was the beginning and end of her ambition. For there was her home; there dwelt her father and mother, brothers and sisters. And there, with his widowed mother, in a little cabin, about a mile up the hill, lived her affianced husband, Dermot Kilfoyle.

Dermot was a big, burly fellow of twenty-five, whose handsome face, browned and burnt by the sun and sea air, told of a warm heart and a quick and somewhat jealous temper. For years he had loved pretty Mave with an adoring love, and when at last she consented to become his wife, his happiness was great.

"Och! begorrah thin, sure it's Dermot that's the fool to be choosin' the likes of her, wid her airs and graces," said the old woman, with a wise shake of her head, as she talked over the match with her cronies. "She'll be afther leadin' him a dance and no mistake."

"Thrue for you," cried another. "But sure, woman alive, the lads do mostly be taken wid a purty face an' a pair of bright eyes."

"Bedad! an' that same's the pity, for there's many's a dacint girl wid a plain face maybe, but wid a heart of gold an' thinkin' of nothin' but doin' her work an' sayin' her prayers that would——"

"Aisy, aisy—it's not many you'll find for him like that. An' sure if you did—a hunderd or so—he'd still fix his eyes on Mave, so you may as well give over."

"Bad manners to it, sure an' I must ; but it's sorry I am to see a fine man like Dermot slootherin' round a girl like Mave, till he doesn't know what he's at."

"Och! well sure he's the dacint lad; an' sure there must be some good in the girl, since he thinks such a hape of her."

But none of these murmurs reached Dermot's ears; and if they had, they would have troubled him little. He was too happy in his new-found bliss.

So for some time all went merrily. Mave was sweet and gentle in voice and manner—glad to receive her lover, and sorry to see him go. She was steady and regular at her work, and not one in the island had a word to say against her.

"Sure there isn't wan like her for miles round, the crathur," Dermot told himself continually. "She's the jewel of a girl entirely, an' she'll make me the happiest man ever stepped, plase the Lord."

But before many months had elapsed, Dermot's peace of mind was disturbed, his soul racked and torn, with wild, unconquerable jealousy. This sudden change in the young man's feelings was brought about in the following manner.

One evening at a dance, when Mave in her neat red petticoat, and blue cotton jacket, a soft white neckerchief folded across her snowy bosom, her pretty feet in their stout little brogues scarcely touching the floor as she tripped gracefully up the middle and down again in time to the music, a stranger appeared suddenly in the doorway and stood looking in, an expression of interest and amusement in his handsome eyes.

The mistress of the cabin, one Mrs. McGurk, stepped forward, and in a hospitable manner invited him to enter.

"My name is Fane—Cecil Fane," he said, following her into the kitchen. "And I'm staying with Dr. Sinclair."

"Sure thin you're welcome as the flowers in May," she said. "The doctor's a rale frind to us all."

Then leading him into the "room," she offered him some refreshment. But both tea and whiskey he politely refused.

"I'll try my hand, or rather my feet, at a jig presently," he said, as he looked back towards the scene of merriment. "There's a lovely girl out there I'd like to ask to teach me how to dance it. Will you kindly present me to her?"

"It's Mave McMahon you mane?" she said. "Och! she'll show you the steps finely."

"I'm sure she will," he answered, smiling. And the next moment he was bowing low before Mave, who, hot and breathless after the last dance, was standing beside Dermot, her hand resting on his arm.

The girl accepted the handsome stranger's invitation to dance with shy reluctance, and blushed deeply as he led her away. For she felt nervous and awkward, knowing full well that every eye in the place was fixed upon her and her partner.

But Fane soon put her at her ease, and in a short

time she was laughing merrily at his energetic attempts to master the jig.

Mave's bright, rustic beauty, her slim, graceful figure, and unusual coloring delighted young Fane, and he took no pains to conceal his admiration.

"I'm an artist," he told her, "and am always in search of a pretty face. May I paint you? Just a little sketch?"

"Sure paint me if you plase," Mave answered with an upward glance of the beautiful eyes. "But you'll have to do me widout seein' me, for sure all day I'm out mindin' the cattle at Torr's Head, beyant."

"Capital!" he cried. "A background of sea and sky is just what I want."

"'Deed thin you'll niver find me," she answered, in a tone that seemed like a challenge. "An' there's many another 'll do just as well."

"Not one. And I'll find you never fear," he said, as, pressing her hand warmly, he bade her good-night. "I'm not easily daunted, as you'll see by and by."

And find her he did, and without as much trouble as he had expected. So easily indeed, that he fancied the bashful maiden had purposely placed herself in an unusually prominent position. However, he did not mention his suspicions, but, rejoicing openly at his good luck in finding her so soon, set up his easel and canvas, and began to work.

A fortnight passed. And as Cecil Fane went

every day to the hill-side and sat there, painting for several hours, the picture grew apace.

One morning, just as it was well-nigh finished, the young man did not appear, and Mave wondered greatly.

"Sure, I'm hopin' he an' Dermot didn't meet," she thought with sudden terror, as the evening came on. "Dermot was that quare-tempered last night that—Patsey," to the boy sent by her father to relieve her, and now seen sauntering slowly across the field, "will you step out a bit, you gosthoon, an' come on—for sure I'm in a mortial hurry."

And as he ran shouting after a straying cow, she started off at a brisk pace down the hill.

About a quarter of a mile away, she came suddenly face to face with Cecil Fane.

"Whither so fast, sweet Mave?" he cried. "I was just going to look for you."

"Oh! sir—sure——" she grew rosy red, "I——"

"You're not in a hurry? Good. Well, then, since you've got rid of your cows, and I've turned my back on my paints, we'll go for a walk." And he led the way towards the sea.

Mave followed him without a word. Her heart beat quickly, and her conscience was ill at ease. She felt she was doing wrong, knew she was wanted at home for many reasons, and trembled at the thought of what Dermot might do or say when he heard of her conduct.

"But there can't be much harm in goin', an' sure it won't be for long," she thought. "An' Dermot's not me master yet."

"This is really delightful," said Fane, little suspecting what a battle was going on in the girl's mind. "It's quite a new sensation to walk about with you, and I must say the sea air agrees with you. It has given you a wondrous color. How I wish I could paint it. But it is, alas! beyond me."

Mave answered nothing, and went along shyly, with downcast eyes, wishing she had courage to go, yet too much fascinated by his pleasant ways and the sweet softness of his voice and language to do so. He told her endless stories of the gay world from whence he came and to which he would return, and assured her that among the many fair ladies he knew there, not one was as beautiful as she. Mave looked at him from under her long lashes, and the color deepened in her cheek. She did not quite believe him; but being a woman, young and very foolish, she was pleased.

"And yet," he said, smiling, as he saw how eagerly she listened to his compliments, "except as an artist, I care little about beauty—so called. The woman I love and hope to make my wife, sweet Lena Grey, is not handsome, but lovely and lovable, because of the holiness and purity that look out of her eyes."

"I'm glad you've told me," cried Mave impulsively. " God bless you an' her, an' give you all joy an' happiness."

"Thank you; and I hope you and she may meet some day."

"'Deed an' that same's not likely."

"Who knows? And I tell you what, Mave, I'll bring her here on our wedding trip."

"Do," cried Mave gayly, " an' sure we'll have a dance for her an' you. Now, that's a bargain."

"Done," he answered, laughing; and raising her hand, he pressed it to his lips. "Lena will be proud and pleased to know you, I feel sure."

At this moment Dermot Kilfoyle came up the path from the beach, carrying a basket of fish upon his back. He was very wet and tired. He had spent a long day on a tossing, angry sea, and was thinking longingly of Mave and the happy walk they would take together in the moonlight.

"There'll be a storm—a bad storm before mornin'," he said, looking towards the west, where the sun was slowly sinking, like a great ball of fire, into the sea. "God help thim that's out late the night. Mercy on us, who's thim two?" he cried, as his eyes fell upon the girl and her companion. "Why if it isn't Mave an' that gomeral of an artist from England."

Then his handsome face flushed hotly, as Fane raised her hand and softly kissed it.

"How dare he?" he muttered. "An' sure

Mave must have taken lave of her sinses." And, scowling angrily, he strode forward.

As Mave saw him approach, she blushed, grew pale, then blushed again.

Fane noticed the quick change of color, and glanced from her to Dermot, then back at her, and laughed.

"Kilfoyle's a good-looking fellow, but a trifle rude," he said. "Look how he scowls at us. One would think he was angry to see us together. He's a rough specimen, I must say."

Mave trembled a little. It annoyed her to hear him speak so. And yet was he not right? Dermot did look rude, and very uncouth, in his coarse clothes, his basket upon his back, his brows knit together in a frown.

"Mave, come home," he said, going close to her side. "You must not stay here talkin' wid this stranger."

She tossed her head and started away with a look of scorn and annoyance.

"I'll go home whin I plase, Dermot Kilfoyle," she said haughtily. "Go your ways and don't mind me."

Dermot grew white to the lips. He glared angrily at Cecil Fane, then, shrugging his shoulders, laughed a bitter, contemptuous laugh.

"Bedad I'll go. It's not me that would come meddlin' where I'm not wanted. But you'll be afther suppin' sorra wid the spoon of grief, Mave McMahon," he said between his teeth, " or my name's not Kilfoyle."

Then turning away, he tramped on up the hill.

As he disappeared, Mave's mood suddenly changed, and she burst into tears.

"Oh, don't, don't mind him!" cried Fane, surprised and alarmed. "He's an insolent fool, and——"

"Arrah, thin, in the name of Heaven say nothin' agin him," she sobbed, "for sure I've promised to be his wife." And she ran past him, down among the rocks, and soon vanished out of sight.

"Poor child! So that's the way the wind blows. Well, I'm sorry—very sorry for you, and bitterly regret having roused the fellow's jealousy. If the picture were but finished, I would go. And he would soon forgive and forget. But, by Jove! at all risks I must have another sitting. Perhaps I might find her on the beach and ask her about to-morrow." And humming softly to himself he went quickly after her.

But Mave was nowhere to be seen.

"Gone home, I suppose," he thought. "Well, let's hope that she and her future lord and master have met and made it up. By Jove! I hadn't an idea of such a thing or I'd have been more careful. I'll give it to Sinclair for not telling me. See if I don't." And seating himself upon a big stone, he began to fill his pipe.

Presently he saw Mave walking towards him along the beach, Dermot Kilfoyle by her side. He had got rid of his creel of fish, and had changed his clothes, but his temper had not softened apparently, for he was talking and gesticulating in an angry, excited way.

Mave's face was flushed and proudly sullen. Her bosom rose and fell quickly, and she seemed to suffer intense emotion. But she held her head high, and kept it turned resolutely away from her lover.

"Come," cried Kilfoyle, as they paused in front of Fane without noticing him, " promise niver to speak to that man agin, and I'll forgive you."

"'Deed thin I'll promise no such thing. I'll spake to any wan I plase—an' Mr. Fane's a gintleman, who——"

"A gintleman, aye," Dermot laughed bitterly, " who mocks an' makes game of you——"

The girl turned upon him with flashing eyes.

"How dare you spake so ! He only says kind an' pleasant things an'——"

He caught her arm in a grasp like a vice.

"An' you—you listen to him—smile on him—you——"

"I'll listen to him, an' to any wan I plase," she cried, wrenching herself free. "I'm not your wife to——"

"No; nor niver will be. I've done wid you, Mave McMahon. So you may talk an' walk wid him till Doomsday." And he strode away from her side, his brain whirling, his heart filled with bitterness and anger.

Mave stood where he had left her, staring out at the great foaming waves. Her blue eyes had an angry light in them, while her rosy lips were pressed tightly together with a look of hard, uncompromising determination.

"He'll come back," she muttered, "an' be sorry for his words. But sure he'll have to be mighty humble entirely, or I'll niver give in." Then, turning suddenly, she saw Cecil Fane seated upon a rock close by.

"Mave," he said, going forward to meet her, "I'm sorry that my friendship should have caused you such trouble. But the picture will soon be finished, and then I'll leave this forever. One more sitting will——"

"I can't give it, sir." Mave had grown very white. "I daren't vex him more. I'm sorry, for sure——"

"Not give it? But think," he caught her hand, "what it means to me."

"It manes more to me sure. But——"

"You'll come? On the hill-side again to-morrow. Good——"

At this moment a boy came running along the beach carrying a telegram.

"Mr. Fane, sir, this came by the packet just now."

"For me?" Fane tore open the envelope, and as he read the message his face blanched, and, in a voice full of emotion, he cried aloud:

"Lena ill—in danger. My God! Then I must leave this to-night. When does the packet sail?" he asked, turning to the messenger.

"Sure, it won't go till mornin'."

"Then I must go in a boat."

"Begorrah, thin, you'll get no boat to take you across the night. It's too stormy; an' sure any man can see that it's gettin' worse it is."

"I must leave the island as soon as possible. Who'd be most likely to take me across?"

"I will." Dermot Kilfoyle stepped up to him, with a white, set face. "I've a boat that 'd sail in any say, an' the wind 'll be wid us," he cried. "So come on, an' lose no time. Not that I wouldn't brave any storm to get shut of you."

A cry of anguish escaped from Mave.

"No, Dermot." She clasped her hands round his arm. "Look at the say. There's a storm comin'."

But he flung her from him. "It's frettin' you are to see him go," he sneered. "You'll be lonesome the morra——"

"No, no, Dermot, but you——"

"Don't consarn yourself about me. There's not many wantin' me—an' I might as well go to the bottom as not. Come on, Misther Fane; the sooner we go—the sooner we'll get it over." And casting a glance of withering scorn and defiance at the trembling girl, he took Fane's arm and dragged him away.

"My God! an' I," she shuddered, "have done this. Driven him—to danger—maybe to death. For there's nothin' will gainsay him now, nothin' 'll turn him back—an' the storm is comin' up—the say just frightenin'."

She pushed back the hair from her brow, and a low, deep moan escaped her lips. Then, scarcely knowing where she went, she began to grope her way among the rocks. But she made but little progress, as every moment she turned and looked out wildly over the ocean.

The evening had now closed in; the rain that had been threatening all day came down in torrents, and a thick mist soon enveloped both sea and land. Blindly Mave staggered along, her heart full of anguish, her soul torn with remorse. The wind howled and shrieked as though in mockery of her grief, and huge waves dashed violently against the rocks, drenching her with their spray.

"Merciful God, have pity," she moaned, "save thim. Holy Mary, Star of the Say, pray for thim. I'm sorry an' repint bitterly of my pride an' wickedness that druv poor Dermot out the night. Ochone!" she gave a cry of terror as through the drifting rain and heavy mist she saw a light, now rising upon the crest of the wave, now engulfed and hidden from sight. That light she knew was in a boat, and in that boat were the two men, Dermot Kilfoyle and Cecil Fane.

"The Lord save an' deliver thim," she gasped. "Sure they're lost. No boat could live in such a say, an' I—God forgive me—I druv thim out to death to-night. O Dermot, Dermot, if I was only by your side!" Then, white and haggard, she struggled up over the rocks, and staggered away along the dark, wet road to her father's cabin.

All through the long hours of the night Mave lay tossing from side to side, in open-eyed misery.

"Maybe the mornin' will bring hope," she murmured, as the storm abated. "An' sure good news may come wid the dawn." And at last, weary and exhausted, she fell into a troubled sleep.

But the next day passed, and when evening came on, no word from Dermot or Fane had reached their friends on the island.

"They're gone fur sure," said one old fisherman, in husky tones. "We'll niver see thim more."

And when the news was spread abroad, that the outgoing packet, that morning, had seen a boat bottom upwards, floating out to sea, all agreed that he was right. There could no longer be any doubt as to what their end had been.

To describe Mave's sorrow, her heart-broken remorse, and bitter self-reproach would be impossible. No one guessed one-half of what she suffered. She did not fall ill, or give way to violent grief, but went about in a half-dazed condition, dry-eyed and silent, the soft bloom in her cheeks slowly fading, the lines round her sweet mouth gradually hardening.

One rainy day, chance took her past the little cabin where Dermot Kilfoyle had lived with his mother. Through the open door she saw the old woman sitting alone, her hands clasped together as though in prayer.

With a sudden stab at her heart she paused and looked in. Then remembering that she had caused this sorrow, she ran up to her, and threw her arms round her neck.

"It's desolit you look, Mrs. Kilfoyle," she cried, bursting into tears, " rale desolit."

"Aye, my dear, for sure Dermot's gone from me. But it's God's will, alanna. An' we must all bow to that. I loved my boy—maybe too well. An' the Lord took him. It's hard, sore hard. But God knows best. An' we must pray for his sowl, Mave. You don't forget that?"

"No. But can you forgive me? Sure 'twas I, druv him from you, in my pride an' vanity I——"

"Whisht, alanna,—an' don't be frettin' too much about that. There was, I've no manner of doubt, faults on both sides. Dermot had always a misfortunit temper, poor lad." Tears rolled down her wrinkled cheeks. "But sure, if he's dhrownded the Lord will forgive you because of your great sorrow; 'twas for sinners He died, Mave. An' He'll have mercy on Dermot, for he was a good son."

"God love you," whispered Mave. "You've put hope into my heart. But till the day of my death I'll niver forgive myself. Only for me he'd niver have gone to say that night."

"Who knows?" sighed the mother. "He was always darin' an' thought greatly of his boat. She was the fine sailer. An' thin when Misther Fane— Och, 'twas the black day brought him among us."

"He was no ways to blame," cried Mave, blushing. "An' sure there'll be many frettin' sore for him."

"Musha, thin, thrue for you. He'd a mother, too, may be?"

"Yes. An' some one who loved him dear. He was thinkin' of marryin' soon, an' now——"

"God comfort thim an' us," said the old woman solemnly. "At such a time He is our only refuge. His holy will be done."

"Amen," sobbed Mave. "But sure it's desolit we all are entirely."

And then they sat, with clasped hands, silently weeping.

From that hour Mave spent every spare moment of the day and night with the lonely woman. Her holy submission to the Divine Will, her gentle and tender way of speaking, touched the girl and soothed her breaking heart. Constant intercourse with her, showing as it did how terrible the loss of her son had been to her, deepened, if possible, Mave's feeling of remorse, and blaming herself for having caused her so much sorrow, she did all she could to console and comfort her. Such sweet sympathy and devotion were very dear to Mrs. Kilfoyle, and before long they became like mother and daughter.

It was a wild autumn that year, and a wilder winter. Terrible storms raged continually, and owing to the almost impassable state of the sea there was but little coming and going between the island and the mainland.

"It's not much we know of what's passin' in the world," remarked Mave one day, as she and Mrs. Kilfoyle sat knitting by the fire. "What wid the desperate wind an' Docther Sinclair bein' away, it's lost we are for news."

"Musha, thin, an' what news would you be wantin', honey?"

"Sure I'd like to know how that poor girl Misther Fane loved is gettin' on. Lena Grey he called her. The telegram said she was ill. I wondher did she die."

"When the docther comes back, an' sure that same won't be long, he'll be able to tell you, may be. He was the only one knew anything of Misther Fane an' his people."

A tall, broad-shouldered man stood in the doorway, and they rose to their feet, in a flutter of surprise and pleasure, as they recognized Dr. Sinclair.

"Well, Mrs. Kilfoyle, I hope I see you well," he cried in a cheery voice. "And Mave McMahon, too—but looking white and thin. We must bring the roses back to your cheeks, my girl." And he laid his hand caressingly upon her shoulder.

Mave grew crimson, and tears rushed to her eyes.

"You're nervous," he said, looking at her with kindly interest, "and run down. We must take care of you and strengthen you before——" He paused abruptly, and seating himself in front of Mrs. Kilfoyle, crossed one leg slowly over the other, saying: "You've never asked me about my visit to England, or any of the things I've seen or heard."

"Och, no, Doether dear, but sure you must have seen hapes of wonderful things."

"Yes," taking a pinch of snuff. "And the last and most wonderful thing—was a wedding."

"A wedding!" the old woman laughed. "Arrah, sure they're common enough—over there especially."

"Yes, so they are. But this one was peculiar —peculiar in this way. The bride and the bridegroom were both on the point of death—or at least, in danger of death some four months ago. The bride through a fall from her horse; the bridegroom through the upsetting of a boat on a tempestuous sea, not very far from the island of Innisboffin. He was found clinging to the boat, and rescued by a passing vessel bound for America. He was safely landed at the first port; but there he fell ill. For some time his life hung in the balance, and he'd probably have died unknown and among strangers, had it not been for a good, devoted fellow, an Irishman, who tended and nursed him with infinite devotion. But thanks to him, his youth, and a good constitution, he recovered, after some time reached home, and was last week married to sweet Lena Grey."

"Docther"—Mave started forward with quivering lips and heaving bosom—"sure it must be about Misther Fane you're tellin' us. If he was saved—what—became of Dermot?"

"My dear child, they were together. Both clung to the boat; both were saved; Dermot it was who nursed and took care of poor Fane. Dermot is alive and well."

"My God!" The old woman threw her arms above her head. "Blessed be Thy holy name forever," she cried in a loud voice; then fell back sobbing upon her seat.

For an instant a look of intense joy lit up Mave's beautiful face, but it passed quickly away, and she grew suddenly pale as death.

"Dermot saved—Dermot alive and well," she moaned in a voice of anguish. "Oh! can it be—can it be true? I have grieved—his mother has shed bitter tears thinkin' him dead, an' he has left us widout a word. Och! it was cruel—downright cruel of him."

"'Deed an' he might have been afther sendin' us

a bit of a letter, just to let us know he wasn't lyin' dhrownded dead," cried the old woman. "But sure there's many mishaps wid the post an'——"

"That's just it," said Dr. Sinclair. "Dermot assured me he had written many letters, telling you that he was alive, and asking Mave's forgiveness—saying he knew the truth about Mr. Fane, who was now his best friend, and that he loved her more than ever, and only waited till she sent him a line to allow him to come home."

"Sure no letter iver came to us," said Mave, with quivering lips.

"Well, Dermot is not much of a scholar, and dear knows what sort of addresses he put on those letters of his. But you see, after all, it was not his fault that you did not know that he was living and well. So don't be too hard, Mave. The poor fellow has suffered terribly. For, not getting any answer from you, he thought you had ceased to care for him, and was very miserable."

"How could he think so?" cried Mave, now rosy red. "Sure he knows nothin' on airth could iver change me."

"That's right," cried the doctor, beaming with delight, as he got up, and walking over to the door opened it wide. "And if I were you," standing upon the step, "I'd tell that without delay to Dermot Kilfoyle himself."

"Oh!" she said with a smile and sigh, "sure if I got the chanst I wouldn't be long doin' that same."

"And if he came to you—just walked in—you'd welcome and be pleased to see him?"

"Oh!" the beautiful eyes filling up with tears, "I'd welcome him from the bottom of me heart. Let him only come, docther, an' thry."

"Do you mane that, Mave, asthore?" asked a voice that sent the blood coursing quickly through her veins, and made her heart beat joyfully. "Oh! me jewel of a girl, put your hand in mine, an' say you love an' forgive me."

"'Deed thin I do, Dermot," she cried, raising a radiantly happy face to his, as she clasped his hand and drew him into the cabin. "I both love you an' forgive you. An' sure there's some one else in here longin' to do the same."

And the next moment Dermot was sobbing like a child upon his mother's breast.

ROSA MULHOLLAND.

ROSA MULHOLLAND was born in Belfast, Ireland, and is the second daughter of the late Joseph Stevenson Mulholland, M.D., of Belfast, and Maria, his wife. Mr. William Mulholland, Queen's Counsel, London, Bencher of Lincoln's Inn, is her brother, and her elder sister is Lady Russell of Killowen, wife of the Lord Chief Justice of England. Miss Clara Mulholland, author of many charming stories, is her younger sister. In 1891 Rosa Mulholland married Mr., now Sir, John T. Gilbert, author of the well-known " History of Dublin " and other standard works relating to Ireland, based on researches among unpublished MSS.

The principal works of Rosa Mulholland (Lady Gilbert) are as follows :

"The Wild Birds of Killeevy," "Marcella Grace," "A Fair Emigrant," "Dunmora," "Hester's History," "The Wicked Woods," "The Squire's Granddaughters," "The Late Miss Hollingford," "Banshee Castle," "Giannetta," "Hetty Gray," "Four Little Mischiefs," "Five Little Farmers," "Puck and Blossom," "The Little Flower-Seekers," "The Walking Trees and Other Tales," "Eldergowan and Other Stories," "The Haunted Organist of Hurly Burly and Other Stories," "Marigold and Other Stories," "Our Own Story and Other Tales," "Vagrant Verses," "Holy Childhood," "The Story of Jesus Simply Told for the Young," "The First Christmas of Our Dear Little Ones," and "Spiritual Counsels for the Young."

Granny Grogan.

BY ROSA MULHOLLAND GILBERT.

BALLYBATTER is a small town a few miles from Dublin city, countryward, to the sea. It has one street with good shops, and it has slums, in which dwell, chiefly, laborers and their families, a few old pensioners, a good many widows and spinsters, who make a great " debate " for life by means of some ill-rewarded industry, and a certain number of idlers who prefer to loaf, and make out existence nobody knows how. Nearly all the women of Ballybatter take in " a bit of washing." Granny Grogan's house was at the very end of Sweeny's Court, and placed so that from the one kitchen of which the " house " consisted a view was obtained of the entire row of dwellings and the stony pavement in front of them. The granny, who was seventy-five years old and bedridden, could see from her bed all that went on in the Court during the day. The pump, which is its central object, was within the range of her vision. Nobody could take a can of water from it without her knowledge, and when Judy Flynn, the most dissipated member of her sex in the whole of Ballybatter, was " afther havin' dhrink taken " and come to sober herself by pumping a shower-bath on her own head, Granny Grogan was the first, and sometimes the only, person to be scandalized at her proceedings. She watched the small children at their play of making dirt-pies in the gutter, and measured time by the return of " laboring boys " to their dinner and the ringing of the Angelus bell from the chapel only a hundred perches away, with its back door open to the slums, and its front entrance facing the highroad where the quality " do be dhrivin' " through Ballybatter on their way to the sea.

The granny was a small woman, shrivelled into half her original size by the rheumatism, which had twisted her poor hands till they looked like the gathered-up claws of a dead bird. She could neither sit up properly nor lie down, and crouched in her bed with her head leaning forward and her chin almost touching her breast. She had lived in this earthen-floored, damp kitchen for many years, and had done her laundry work in it so well that she was known as the best washerwoman in Ballybatter. She had been married to her second husband and taken him to burial from under this roof. Her two sons had walked out of the place to enlist, and she had shed her tears in it over the letter that informed her of their death. Here she still remained, now that she was alone and helpless, her rent paid by a former patron, and her needs supplied from day to day by the occasional doles of the charitable, and the self-denying kindness of the neighbors in the Court. "Run in an' light the granny's fire," a harassed mother of ten would say to her little girl in the morning, and another would pour off the first cup of tea from the cracked teapot on the hob, and carry it to her, saying, "The heart of her would be dyin' within her, the crature, afther the night she does have, an' her neither lyin', nor sittin', nor even standin' up itself!" Rumors that Granny Grogan would be whizzed off to the House (poorhouse) were sometimes afloat, but they were always hushed up, and she held her place from year to year, while it was admitted that "the Court would be quare and lonesome if so be the like of her was ever to be took out of it."

However, one summer when the times were particularly hard, and two or three other old people had disappeared into the Union Hospital, a feeling grew among the more discontented of the slums population that there was no reason why Granny Grogan should be supported among the neighbors when their children wanted bread. The old creature herself heard the whisper and trembled; but still the weeks passed on and nothing was done. The death of the patron who had paid her rent intensified matters, and the landlord's grumbling, growing louder as the defaulting eighteenpences became more and more conspicuous in his monthly accounts, seemed to herald the dreaded winding-up of Mrs. Grogan's career in Sweeny's Court.

"I'm feared it'll have to be the end of it," said

Mrs. Mooney, as she hung her bit of washing on the long line across the Court. She was talking to Mrs. Nolan, who was scraping her stirabout pot on the stones, stopping to hit a couple of hens on their heads with her iron spoon as they dashed at the scrapings, intended for them, with their too-eager bills.

"God help her!" said Mrs. Nolan, "it's a pity the Lord wouldn't take her, and her so ready to go. Sure heaven 'd be a grand change for her afther Sweeny's Court."

"Cock her up with heaven all in a hurry!" said Mrs. Mooney. "Isn't purgatory itself a crowned king to the Union?"

"Take the mug, Katie," said Mrs. Nolan to the little curly-haired child standing by her, "and run an' see if the new American milk-woman will give a sup of milk out of her can for the poor ould woman that lives among the neighbors. I hear she's a plentiful kind of a woman, an' I see her cart-wheel standin' there at the foot o' the lane."

The little girl was beside the milk-cart by the time its owner had got down from her perch.

"Will you give a sup o' milk for Granny Grogan, ma'am?" begged the little one with uplifted blue eyes and outstretched mug.

"Where's your money?" demanded the milk-woman curtly.

"Granny Grogan has no money," lisped Katie, undaunted.

"Och, sure it's the granny that lives among the neighbors," said a bystander. "Everybody gives her a bite and a sup."

"That'll soon all be over with her when she's took to the Union."

"Then I'm sorry if it's comin' to that with her."

The words flew about the American woman's ears, while Katie stood before her all the time staring and persistent. When she had finished her business in the retail milk-shop which she had come to supply, she turned to the child.

"Now, where is your Granny Grogan?" she said abruptly.

"This way, ma'am," cried Katie, and the stranger trudged down the court after her with her clanking milk-cans.

Mary Mallon was a buxom woman with eyes of a warm brown, and with a strong mouth. She looked like a person who would begin big things on impulse and carry them through with determination. A large white apron almost covered her, and her plaid shawl and black bonnet were put on with care. As she passed down the court Granny's neighbors came to their doors and said: "That's the woman that came home from America with money, and has bought 'Bawneen' and set up cows. It's good to go to America a young one, and come back rich afore you're altogether too ould for anything."

Mrs. Mallon had walked to the top of the Court,

and stood in the doorway of Granny Grogan's kitchen, looking in. She saw the little aged cripple crouched in her bed, with her shoulder against the damp wall. The bed, which was set up on a kind of box with legs, was clean, and a number of more or less ragged and smoked religious prints disputed place with the spots of damp on the whitewash, or rather graywash, making an aureole of saints in red and yellow round the old woman's head. Mrs. Grogan's cap was clean, so was the white shawl pinned around her shoulders. There was a little spot of pink in her poor old cheeks, and the twinkling eyes that turned towards the door were as blue and as bright as a baby's. Mrs. Mallon stood still and looked at her steadily for a few moments, and then advanced into the house and deposited her cans with a clank on the earthen floor.

"Haven't ye anything bigger than this?" said the milk-woman to the little girl who was pushing the mug into her hands.

"God bless ye, woman!" said Mrs. Nolan, who, with Mrs. Mooney, had left her own business to follow the stranger. "Katie, run in for the jug, an' be quick with ye!"

Mrs. Mallon turned and faced the two observant matrons.

"She's so like my own gran'mother," she said, and turned again for another long, mild stare at Granny Grogan.

"That's a good while back," said Mrs. Mooney,

with eyes that guessed the probable age of the American.

"She died when I was ten years old, an' that's not yesterday, neither," said Mrs. Mallon. "Forty years ago it is, come Pathrick's mornin'."

"You've the best of a good mimbery," said Mrs. Nolan admiringly.

Mrs. Mallon took the jug from the returning Katie and filled it to overflowing.

"There's more where that came from," she said gently, depositing it on the rickety table by the old woman's side.

"May God's blessin' be about you!" said Granny Grogan. "It's Him that has always got somethin' unexpected to dhrop into the open hand!"

"It's my gran'mother's voice she has, too," said Mary Mallon, taking up her cans.

"Sure one ould woman's a good deal like another," said Mrs. Nolan. "But when ye have such a heart for your own people, ma'am, I suppose ye must be glad to be back in ould Ireland."

"I have no people," said Mary Mallon. "I've been down through the counthry lookin' for them where I left them. They're all dead an' forgotten in their own place, long ago."

She turned and trudged to her cart, put her cans on board, mounted to her seat beside her son who was in charge of it, and drove off out of the town of Ballybatter.

Bawneen was distant about a mile and a half along a by-road which took to the hills, and Mrs. Mallon was at home when she reached a small white gate leading to a good cottage with a rose half covering the whitewash. Behind were a few fields where half a dozen cows were at grass. Young Mallon went round to the back premises with the pony and cart and cans, and his mother walked into the kitchen of her cottage. The interior was neat and bright. Her daughter, a girl of eighteen, welcomed her with smiles.

"You look tired, mother."

"I'm dead bet, Janie. The breath's been took out of me. I seen the ghost of my gran'mother in a lane of Ballybatter."

Janie laughed. "That's some comfort for you, surely, mother, after the search you have been making for your own people."

"It was herself—face an' voice, an' all, an' the very blink of her eyelids up at me."

"I never heard you talk much about your gran'mother," said Janie. "It was always your mother you were thinkin' about."

"I didn't know I remembered my gran'mother at all till I saw their Granny Grogan," said Mrs. Mallon, "and then she flashed up in my mind, the same as if you put a match to a candle. My mother was altogether different. She was tall, an' straight, an' han'some, an' her eyes were brown an' her hair was black. This little crature's eyes are as blue as yours, an' she never could have been big. I see my gran'mother now, as plain as can be, in a little bed like that again' the wall in the corner, an' the voice of her chattin' out to us childher."

"Will you have a cup of tea, mother?"

"I couldn't swallow anythin' just at present. I tell ye, the blankets on that old crature's bed are terrible, an' I felt the pains in my own fingers lookin' at her poor rheumatized hands. I'll want to go down to Donnelly's shop to-morrow to get some warm things an' take them to her."

Janie went to bed that night perplexed at her mother's persistence in dwelling on the recollection of her grandmother; and long after her son and daughter were asleep, and the little house was silent, Mrs. Mallon sat at the fire staring into the coals, and going back as far as memory would carry her into the events of her own earlier life. At fifteen she had been hurried out of her home in an extraordinary and unexpected manner. The little home had stood among the Connemara hills. There, in the heart of the fire, the woman of fifty years could see, as vividly as though she were still living in a far-distant moment of time, the mountain and moorland scene before the cabin door. The chain of hills, dark with evening purple, or glittering in dew and sunshine, filled the background capped with flying clouds. The dazzling green of the bit of wet pasture was at her feet, the mellow coloring and sad shadows of the bogland lay between, and here and there among the mists a mile away the gable of a neighbor's house gleamed. A goat browsed on a bit of green bank, the wind shook the tassels of the alder-bush, stunted by many storms, that sheltered the cabin thatch. On a little causeway of rough stones before the door a few hens were feeding on a potato just broken and thrown to them by a little girl who was standing on the threshold. "*Ora Maury! Mau—ry! Ora Maury!*" cried a voice from a distance, and the child turned and saw her mother, saw her as Mrs. Mallon had described her to her daughter Janie. The mother passed out into the field, and little Mary passed in to attend to her grandmother.

This dream with its pictured figures and echo of voices seemed a life more real to the woman than any she had known in her later years. The vision remained where memory stores up its first prints, impressions sharply bitten in, not to be obliterated by images overlaid upon them. While she stared in the fire the coals fell in, the picture shifted and changed, a burning sun hung over the landscape, and the girl Mary, now grown older, watched a funeral wending along the mountain road, and wept at the cries of the mourners coming to her on the wind. It was the time of the Big Hunger, and she saw her father gasping for death, and her mother wringing her hands by his side. The little children sobbed, and there was no bread and no meal; the potatoes were rotted in the ground. Neighbors came as beggars to the door, and could not find relief. White faces were everywhere, and dead men and women were lying unburied by the roadside.

Mrs. Mallon watched attentively as she saw the girl come out of the house before dawn, and, after a long look back at the cabin, set off running down the road towards the nearest town. It was a long way off, that town, the girl did not know how long, but she had heard that bread could be had there, and her intention was to beg for bread and return with it to the hungry.

She remembered the lifts on carts, the long weary miles of walking, and her uneasiness when the night came down. But her purpose remained undaunted—to reach the town and to procure bread. Arrived in the streets, she was swept away with a crowd pressing towards a vessel which lay in the harbor ready to set sail for America. There on board that ship, said some one, they are giving out bread, and if you go on board you will get it. She went on board. She was weary and bewildered; they gave her some food and a place to rest. But when she thought of returning on shore the vessel had sailed and was a good way out at sea.

Of her struggles and sufferings after she was landed in America Mary Mallon could not bear to think. She escaped some great dangers, she made her way among decent people who procured her respectable employment. She got a letter written home, but it produced no answer. With great determination she applied herself to learn to read and write, and letter after letter was sent home by her to the mountains. At last, one bitter morning, there came a reply. All her people, without exception, had died of the famine. She was an orphan and alone in the world.

Flitting over her years of desolate striving, Mrs. Mallon reviewed her happy married life. Her husband was good to her, and when he died, left her money enough to enable her to remain prosperous with industry. She remembered how after the children were grown up a craving awoke in her, urging her to return to the old land and settle there, maybe to come on the track of some of her father's or mother's people, or even to discover their graves. A year ago she had arrived in Ireland, just thirty-five years since she had sailed from there out of the Big Hunger. Before making up her mind to settle anywhere she had undertaken a pilgrimage to her native mountains. She and her son and daughter had stopped a week in the neighborhood of the spot on which memory assured her that her father's cabin stood. Only a heap of gray stones was on the site. That, she was told, was one of the houses thrown down in the famine year. Sure the people all died that had lived in them, and the only way they had to bury them was to tumble the walls on them!

It was so long ago, so long ago, and yet, as Mary

Mallon sat staring into the fire, tears dropped down her face to think of how she had run out of her mother's sight " unknownt " to get bread, and had never come back. " What did she think o' me, at all, at all ? " whispered Mary to herself. " Or did the death come on her so sudden that she hadn't time to miss me ? "

Then Mrs. Mallon went down on her knees and prayed aloud in the silent house for her dead mother, father, grandmother, brothers, and sisters, and so eased her heart before she lay down to sleep.

When she wakened in the morning her first thought was for Granny Grogan. She sent her son to take round the milk, and soon after walked into Donnelly's shop, where she purchased the best pair of blankets in the place, besides some comfortable woollen garments. With her arms full of these she proceeded down the Court and entered into Granny Grogan's kitchen. Before any one could follow she had seized the little old cripple in her strong embrace, dressed her in the new warm clothing, and wrapped her up in the blankets. The matrons of Sweeny's Court were, at the moment, occupied in their own houses or visiting round the corner hearing the particular morning news of Daly's Lane. Mrs. Mallon had the granny's kitchen all to herself for an hour. She made a pot of good tea, and boiled an egg, and cut a plateful of fresh bread and dainty butter.

"I had a gran'mother once of my own," she said, as she served the meal, "and I'm goin' to call you Granny."

"You may call me what you plaze, my dear, but you're too ould to be my gran'daughter," the old woman said with her twinkling upward smile, from a bent face that could not be uplifted.

"I was young and small when my granny was the same as you," said Mrs. Mallon. "She was my mother's mother, an' as like you as two peas in a pod. Have you got no gran'childher of your own, Granny Grogan?"

"Sorra chick nor child. All of the childher died on me. None of them lived to be married, neither, so how could I have gran'childher, dear?"

"How long have you been livin' in this Court, Granny Grogan?"

"Ever since I came here with my second husband, dear. He wasn't as good a man as the first—God be merciful to them both; but we can't have everything."

"Were you ever in the country where the mountains and fields do be?"

"Was I, is it? Oh, then, heavenly Father, didn't I live an' die there? Sure my heart is buried in it, an' it's only a dead woman I am ever since I left it."

"What part of the country did ye live in?"

"Did ye ever hear tell o' the Twelve Pins of Connemara?"

"Wasn't I down there thravellin' about a month or two ago?"

"For God's sake! An' will ye tell me if the hills is where they used to be all them long, long years ago, acushla? Sure the Irish comes on me tongue again when I think o' them. Och! it's me that was oncet the happy woman carryin' home the turf from the bog an' sweepin' out me house with a broom made o' the beautiful heather. An' the potatoes growin' in at the dure, an' the larks singin' up in the clouds just fit to deave ye."

"Woman alive! Why did ye ever lave it?"

"Och! dear, I didn't lave it with a light heart, I can assure ye, an' that not till me husband an' me childher died of the Black Hunger on me, and meself left for dead, an' nearly buried along with them. I don't know how I crawled away from it all an' made me way up here, an' pulled meself together again. But sure it wasn't me at all that was in it, afther, only a poor cracked crature that had to put in a year in an asylum afore me head came right again."

Mary Mallon left the fireside and came and sat down by the bed.

"It's no wonder I took to ye," she said, "for meself remembers the Black Hunger well."

"You're hardly ould enough, dear."

"I was young at the time, of course."

"I niver heard of any of your name where I came from," said Mrs. Grogan.

"An' I disremember your name in the place where I was."

"Did your gran'mother that you do be talkin' about die in the Hunger, alanna?"

"Sure the grass was growin' on her years afore that. It was me mother that died in it—me mother and me father, an' me sisters an' me brothers. Only meself got away to America out of it."

"You're not like me," said Granny Grogan, "ye thruv well out of it. It came at the young end o' your life. But ye have the heart that desarves to prosper. Look at all this that ye've been doin' for me!"

After that the tie between the Irish-American and Granny Grogan became closer every day. Two or three times a week Mrs. Mallon was in the granny's kitchen, taking her milk, or eggs, or tea, or some other comfort to make her life of pain less irksome. At last there came a day when she arrived and found an unusual commotion in the Court. The crowd that had gathered at its opening fell back and made way when the large figure and strong, intelligent face of Mary Mallon were seen approaching.

"What's all this about?" asked Mrs. Mallon.

"Och, sure, it's what they're come to take Granny Grogan to the poorhouse, God help her! The lan'lord wants her house."

"Haven't I paid her rent for her this month past, faithful?" said Mrs. Mallon indignantly.

"You did, jewel. But, ye see, there's a dale of errors due," said Mrs. Nolan, who had forced herself to the front.

"An' they say the lan'lord's goin' to pull down the house an' make it habitationable," said another neighbor.

"Isn't there any place else to be had?" asked Mary Mallon.

"Plenty," said some one, "only nobody will let a place to a desticute ould crature like the likes o' her."

Mrs. Mallon's face showed all its strongest lines, and she shut her mouth, and pushed her way up to the top of the Court. Sure enough, preparations were being made for conveying Granny Grogan to the Union.

One or two officials were in the little kitchen and a vehicle stood at the door. Mrs. Mallon went in, and the little weak eyes of the old creature in the bed glinted up at her with a watery smile in them.

"You see it's the will o' God, acushla!" she said, with a piteous attempt at cheerfulness. "Ye did what ye could for me. All of yez was good to me. But His Majesty himself has sent for me. Why but I would go?"

Mrs. Mallon turned to the officials.

"Clear out of this," she said in a loud, ringing voice.

"Sorry not to oblige ye, ma'am," said the foremost man, who was about to lift the old woman, blankets and all, out of her bed into the conveyance outside.

"Clear out o' this, I tell yez," said Mary Mallon, and she suddenly seized the man, who was but a small specimen of his sex, in her strong arms, whirled him outside the door, and placed him standing on the pavement.

"An assault!" shrieked the official. "Ye'll pay for this, ma'am!"

"Be off out o' the place, or it's salted ye'll be in airnest," shouted Mrs. Mallon. "But don't be afeard but what ye'll get yer dirty kitchen! Sure it's rotted to death the crature is in it these years past. Here, Katie, run for a cab for me, an' get the best one, an' the comfortablest one ye can clap yer eyes on!"

By this time the crowd was round the door, and every one was pushing to get a sight of what was going on within Granny's kitchen. Mrs. Mooney came struggling out from the interior, "dunching" with her elbows till she placed herself where she wanted to be.

"Yez may as well be off," she said to the officials. "She gives ye lave to summons her tomorrow. Yez can bring her before the Queen if ye like. An' may I niver see the light of heaven if I don't think she's goin' to take Granny Grogan home with her this minnit to her own place!"

A chorus of exclamations greeted this speech,

and even the insulted official left off fuming, and stared with open mouth at Mrs. Mooney.

"Ye'd betther drive off in your kyerridge, the pair of yez!" continued Mrs. Mooney sarcastically. "There's a betther convaynience busy waitin' to step up to the dure."

Curiosity to see what was about to happen overpowered all other feelings in the official mind, and they made way for the cab which now came up the Court, with little Katie's smutty face grinning in delight through the window. A very few minutes saw Mrs. Mallon's intention fulfilled. She carried out the granny, and placed her in the cab as if she had been a baby, and drove off with her amid the cheers of the bystanders. No sooner had the crowd realized what had happened than numbers set off to run after the cab, and to assure themselves that the thriving American dairy-woman had taken bodily possession of Granny Grogan. Even the outraged officials followed meekly, and forgot their wrongs in sympathy with the general enthusiasm. When, finally, they saw the granny hoisted out of the cab, and disappearing through the cottage doorway, they set up such a cheer as brought Mary Mallon out to her little wicket to say a word of good-by for the granny to the neighbors.

"She'll niver forget your kindness. She's thankful to the whole of ye," said Mary Mallon, the strong face lighting up with a broad smile. "An' yez needn't be frettin' any more about the crature, for it's meself that is goin' to take the best o' good care of her."

Meanwhile Granny Grogan had been deposited on Mrs. Mallon's bed in her own room, a pleasant little spot with a cheap yellow paper on the wall, giving it a sunny aspect, with a comfortable piece of carpet on the floor, and neat white curtains on the window, the sill of which was gay with wall-flowers. The bed was one of luxury to the poor old creature, who kept murmuring alternately incoherent prayers and ejaculations of amazement.

When Mrs. Mallon turned into the house again she directed her daughter Janie to make a cup of tea and carry it to Granny Grogan. Being somewhat in need of refreshment herself, she was about raising a tea-cup to her lips when she heard something that stayed her hand and caused her to throw up her face with a look of wonder and excitement.

The sound that had startled her was of a voice, high-pitched, clear, sweet, crying as if to some one at a distance.

"*Ora Maury—Mau-ry! Ora Maury!*"

Janie came out of the inner room smiling, but stood still in surprise as her eyes fell on her mother.

"What is it?" she said. "Mother, what's the matter with you?"

"I heard my mother's voice callin' me," said Mary Mallon, staring at her.

"Why, it was only Granny Grogan, poor old creature. The moment she set eyes on me she opened her mouth and set up that extraordinary screeching."

Mrs. Mallon sat down at the table and leaned her head on her hand. "I wonder what is on me at all, at all?" she said helplessly.

"That old woman has bewitched you," said Janie.

Mrs. Mallon got up and went slowly across the kitchen into the inner room. There she found Granny Grogan shaking and trembling in the bed, with tears dropping down from her poor old eyes all over the quilt.

"What on airth is aildin' you, granny dear?" said Mrs. Mallon.

"O holy Mother o' God! O Vargin Mother, isn't it the ghost o' my young girsha that is afther walkin' in to me! Ora, what sort of a place is this at all, at all? Is it heaven ye brought us to, whin my Maury is in it—the daughter that wint out from me one mornin' an' niver came back?"

"Didn't ye tell me that yer childher all were dead since the year o' the Hunger?" said Mary Mallon, beginning to shake and tremble also.

"An' what but death would ha' kept my girsha from comin' back to me? Sick with the hunger she was like the rest of us, an' she died on the mountain or in the bogs without a Christian to spake to her. Sure her grave is in my heart, but sorra 'nother grave do I know of that iver you were laid in, my gra gal machree, Mary O'Shaughnessy!"

Mrs. Mallon uttered a sharp cry. "How could your daughter be Mary O'Shaughnessy, Granny Grogan?"

"How? Because she was Denis O'Shaughnessy's child, an' him her father, an' why else? Denis O'Shaughnessy, the husband o' my youth, alanna, asthore machree! Sure I niver was Grogan until sorra had batthered and twishted me into somebody that wasn't the like o' me at all, at all!"

Mary Mallon stood for a few moments with her face hidden in her hands, and her intelligent brains at work thinking something out. Presently she sat down beside the agitated old woman and put a strong arm round the crippled shoulders.

"Mother!" she said—"Mother! I am really your daughter, Mary O'Shaughnessy."

"*You*, Mrs. Mallon? Oh, no, dear. You're good enough to be a daughter to me, but my daughter was a young girsha. And the eyes of her were blue, an' the hair of her was brown an' light an' curly. Oh, vo! didn't I see the ghost of her a minute ago, smilin' at me, an' smilin' at me with the very heart's blood of the smile that she did always have for me?"

"Mother, that girl is *my* daughter. She's maybe like what I was when I quit out an' left you. Sure I mind it all as well as if it were yesterday. Ye were standin' over my father, an' him lyin' on the floor.

You said 'twas only bread would cure him, an' somebody told me there was bread givin' out in the town. An' when I got to the town they told me there was bread on the ship. An' when I got to the ship they sailed out to sea with me. An' people wrote out to me that the whole o' you were dead. An' I lived my life in America till last year, when the longin' riz up in me to come back to the old country. An' then I sthravaigned into Sweeny's Court with my milk-cans, an' I saw you lookin' the image of my gran'mother. It's the years that has done it on the whole of us, ye see. They turned you into a likeness of your own mother—that's *my* granny—and they brought up my Janie to be the moral of *her* mother—that's myself—as I was when yourself last lost sight o' me, mother avourneen!"

It was long before Granny Grogan was able to understand the state of affairs, but when at last she was made to realize that her own daughter and grandchildren were around her the joy and excitement of it all nearly cost her her life. After some time, however, she grew accustomed to the happiness that had come to her, and for the rest of her days was an object of devotion to her family, and of extraordinary interest to the kindly neighbors of old who had been so good to her in Sweeny's Court.

MRS. BARTLE TEELING.

Mrs. Bartle Teeling (née Theodora Louisa Lane Clarke) was born in Guernsey, but passed her childhood in Woodeaton, Oxford, where her father was Rector. On his death his widow returned with their only child to Guernsey, and became there a centre of literary and scientific interest and mental activity as student and writer of natural history, etc., and author of several scientific manuals.

Mrs. Lane Clarke was a strong Protestant, but her daughter, the subject of this sketch, after years of anxious thought and deep but solitary research, for she had not a single Catholic acquaintance, was received into the Church.

Shortly after her conversion, while she was still under twenty-one, she made her first essay in literature, at the request of Father Lockhart, in *The Lamp*, of which he was editor.

Her marriage, which was solemnized by Father Lockhart, was the first marriage which took place in the historic church of St. Etheldreda since " the Reformation."

Since the death of her mother, whom she had the happiness of bringing into the Church, Mrs. Teeling has published some fifty articles and biographical sketches in *The Month, Temple Bar, The Catholic World, The Gentleman's Magazine*, and other publications.

Although she has seven young children and all the cares of a household, scarcely a month passes that she has not an article in at least one of the many magazines to which she contributes

Her Last Stake.

BY MRS. BARTLE TEELING.

CHAPTER I.

It was only the month of May; yet the season was already almost August-like in its sultry heat, and shops were beginning to put up their shutters with the customary notice, "Ouverture le 1re Octobre," and hotel omnibuses to convey huge mountains of trunks and portmanteaux to, instead of from, the unpretending little railway station which, like all its fellows, has welcomed so many illustrious strangers to the Riviera.

Just as the day was at its hottest, and the "butterflies of fashion," as some one calls them, had presumably folded their wings to rest until sundown—for few, if any, were to be seen flitting in and out of the gorgeous hotels which seem to constitute modern Mentone—two slender, black-robed figures advanced somewhat timidly up the footpath leading to one of the largest of these, and, after a brief parley with the porter, were ushered into a large and luxuriously furnished salon.

To them there entered, after a few minutes' delay, a quiet-looking, middle-aged lady with gray hair and placid expression, who cast an inquiring glance upon her visitors as she advanced with a little bow towards them.

"You speak English?" she inquired hesitatingly, as the two nuns rose to receive her.

"We *are* English," was the unexpected reply from the elder of the two, given in rich, round tones; "that is to say, we are Irish."

"Irish? Oh!" and the lady's face brightened as she held out both hands to the visitors. "Irish nuns? What an unexpected, welcome sight!" she went on, drawing a chair close to them. "Where did you come from, and how came you here?"

"Indeed, it doesn't seem the place for us, does it?" laughed the nun. "I never felt more out of my element. But the fact is, we are on a begging tour."

"What Order do you belong to?" asked Mrs. Mortimer, glancing at their black habits and white coifs as if seeking some indication which might guide her. "Nazareth Nuns, Little Sisters of the Poor, Sœurs de Nevers—you seem to look a little like each, and yet to be unlike all."

"Well, we are a new nursing order, founded not many years ago—our foundress still lives—with houses in England and in Italy; and we have been sent out from the latter country to collect subscriptions all along this line."

"Principally from the English visitors, I suppose?"

"Well, yes; for we are not very strong in French, either of us." And the good-tempered Irishwoman smiled across to her companion in placid contentment with her own linguistic shortcomings. So they chatted on for awhile of their houses, their Order, and their work; and then they rose to go, as Mrs. Mortimer pulled out her purse.

"Here is my little offering, sisters," she said, as she laid a small gold piece in Sister Raphael's hand. "I wish it were more, for I feel quite interested in your work; but you know even a quiet, lone body like myself has many calls on the purse."

"Do you stay here long?" asked Sister Raphael of her, just, as it seemed, for the sake of conversation as she ushered them across the big, palm-decked hall.

"I have been here all the winter for my health, but I am leaving to-morrow. By the bye, how did you come to hear of me?" she asked, stopping short in the middle of the hall with an amused glance back at them.

"Oh! we manage to hunt up all the English names everywhere—you are the only English person now in this hotel, are you not?"

"Yes. There are still a good many people here,

but none of them English—except—ah, yes——"
She stopped short as she caught sight of two men advancing towards them, who were whispering gravely and earnestly together.

"*Bon jour*, Monsieur Grosjean," she called out pleasantly to one of the two—a big, heavy-looking Frenchman, who was knitting his brows and biting his lips in evident perplexity as his companion talked. "How does *Monsieur le Médecin* find his patient to-day?"

Monsieur Grosjean, who in fact was no less than the proprietor of the hotel, advanced towards the little group, slowly shaking his head.

"Ah, madame, it is a terrible business—a dreadful thing indeed, for me."

"What, is she worse?" said Mrs. Mortimer quickly.

"*Monsieur le Médecin* will tell you," he replied, with a theatrical gesture towards his companion.

"What is the matter with the lady at number 27?" asked Mrs. Mortimer of the vivacious-looking little doctor, who was drawing on his gloves.

With a glance at the hotel proprietor, which was answered by an affirmative nod, the doctor pronounced "Typhus fever, madame, of the most virulent type——"

"But, O madame, I implore you, let it not be known among my *pensionnaires!*" breathed the proprietor; "it would ruin—simply ruin my hotel."

"And the worst of it is, that there is not a nurse to be had; I can't have my patient left to die alone," muttered the doctor discontentedly.

"Your own compatriot, madame," murmured M. Grosjean, turning his big black eyes plaintively upon Mrs. Mortimer, as though he sought to transfer the burden of responsibility from his own shoulders to hers.

All this time the two nuns had stood patiently apart under the palm-boughs, wondering whether they might slip quietly out and so take their departure, or whether Mrs. Mortimer had any more last words to say.

"Well, monsieur, if she *is* my compatriot I can hardly be expected to nurse her myself, can I? Oh! stay, though," she went on, as her eyes fell upon the waiting pair; "look here, these nuns are English nursing sisters: suppose you set one of them to nurse the sick lady?"

"Nurses, are they?" exclaimed the little doctor; and he darted quickly to their side and broke into voluble explanations and entreaties. The sisters turned to Mrs. Mortimer in utter bewilderment.

"My dear sisters, yes—indeed it is most urgent. You have just been telling me that your work is to nurse the sick in their own homes, rich and poor alike; to go wherever you are summoned, irrespective of creed or position, and without fixed fee. Here is a case which calls for charity as loudly as any. A poor lady, staying at this hotel all the winter, has been taken ill with typhus fever, and now lies unconscious up-stairs. No nurse can be found to undertake the case; and I fancy the proprietor does not care to make himself responsible for the payment and maintenance of one of the expensive style of English nurses who are the only ones to be found hereabouts. But no doubt the lady's friends will come forward later, when they can be communicated with."

The sisters hesitated, and then began to consult together in low tones, the youngest nun apparently objecting, and the elder urging her arguments. Presently the latter, Sister Raphael, turned to Mrs. Mortimer, the proprietor and doctor both standing expectantly aside.

"I think," said Sister Raphael, "that it seems as if we ought to do something for the poor lady. But, you see, we cannot definitely undertake the case without orders. I propose that Sister Gabrielle here should remain with the patient for a few days, while I continue my journey homewards, as I have business to transact *en route*, and meanwhile we can write to our Mother for further orders."

"Any help, even for a day or two, will be most welcome, I am sure," said Mrs. Mortimer; and she repeated the proposal to the two men, who immediately turned to Sister Raphael with profuse expressions of gratitude.

"We had better go to the patient at once," then

said Sister Raphael; and the little doctor turned to accompany them up-stairs and install his new-found nurse.

"O sister, my heart fails me—indeed it does!" whispered Sister Gabrielle, as they followed him up the wide marble staircase. "It's not the nursing I am afraid of, but being alone in this great big place, and not a soul to speak to in my own language."

"Now, Gabrielle dear, you mustn't speak like that. Sure, Our Lady will take care of you."

"Yes, I know," somewhat plaintively assented the younger. "But I haven't got any of my nursing things, you know—aprons, sleeves, and so on. If—if—I stay, will you write for some for me?"

"I'll settle all that, never fear!" said cheery Sister Raphael. "I wish I could stay myself, but you know I am bound to go back with all the money and business letters and accounts to Mother."

So they mounted beyond the "*première étage*," and higher still beyond the "*deuxième*," and finally passed along the corridor and paused at a door before which hung a white sheet duly soaked in disinfectants.

"I have put that up already, you see," remarked the doctor, touching it. "Dangerous thing to do, though—might arouse suspicion—told the chambermaid it was to keep out draughts."

He lifted it for them to pass, and they went on into the sick-room.

A close, sickening odor—the peculiar effluvia of typhus—was the first thing of which they became conscious on entering the apartment. Then they found themselves standing beside the bed whereon lay, tossing and muttering in fevered delirium, a woman of some forty years old, whose thin hands wandered feebly to and fro over the coverlet, while her dark hair, streaked with gray, streamed in tangled masses over a soiled and tumbled pillow. A table beside the bed was crowded with medicine bottles, half-empty cups and glasses, and other paraphernalia of a neglected sick-room; clothes and soiled linen lay upon every chair, and a travelling trunk, dragged into the middle of the room, stood half-open.

"If you will just glance round and see what you are likely to want, I will order it as I go down," remarked the doctor. "And I will look in again this evening—in fact, I think for the future I shall pay my visits only after dark, as the proprietor objects to a doctor being seen too often about the place."

The nuns, after a hasty glance round, mentioned some probable wants: a spirit-lamp, cups, and so on, and then the doctor and Sister Raphael turned to go.

"Good-by, dear sister," whispered the latter; "keep up your heart, and send us news of you soon."

And then Sister Gabrielle found herself alone.

She began by opening the window for a moment, to let in some of the pure fresh air which seemed so sadly needed in that fetid sick-chamber; and then, after one brief, refreshing glance at the glories of sea and sky, mountain and olive-yards, which were spread out before her as she closed the casement, she proceeded to set in order the neglected apartment. The tumbled bedclothes were smoothed, the pillow straightened, with deft and gentle touch; soiled clothes and empty plates and glasses cleared away, and a look of cleanliness and order diffused over everything. By and by a knock came to the door, and a tray was handed in to her with some dinner for herself and a basin of very watery-looking beef-tea for the invalid, with an inquiry as to whether anything further was required for the night. "I am not allowed to go in," whispered the coquettish-looking chambermaid, "but you can ring if you require anything."

Meanwhile the sick woman lay quietly on her narrow bed, tossing her hot hands a little from side to side as though in search of some cool spot whereon to rest them, and muttering faintly unintelligible sentences in French and English from time to time. "There will be no change yet," pronounced the doctor at his evening visit, "so make yourself a bed on the sofa and get some rest; you may need it later on." And so night fell upon the silent room.

CHAPTER II.

The days passed on and still the change, for life or death, delayed its coming. Patient Sister Gabrielle still watched beside her unconscious charge, sometimes slipping outside the heavy curtain of that carbolized sheet which shut them off— she and this stranger together—from the world without, to breathe for a few moments the purer air of the corridor and its open window looking towards the mountains, until the pert chambermaid who waited on them whispered to her that "*M. le Propriétaire* requested that *la sœur* would not show herself outside the room, lest other visitors should suspect illness there." So that even that faint relaxation was taken from her. One morning he sent word to her to come to his bureau; and she went, wondering and somewhat anxious, for she knew that he received his daily report from the doctor, and asked herself wherein she could supplement it.

"*Bon jour, ma sœur;* how goes your patient? The same? No worse, no better? Ah! it is trying, this." He spoke in halting yet not altogether bad English, knowing that the nun's command of French was but slight. "Look here, I have some word to say to you. Have you found, among the lady's possessions, any such things as letters, papers, *hein?*"

"I have not looked, monsieur," replied Sister Gabrielle, with some indignation.

"But it would be well that you should do so," he returned. "Look here: we must find out her friends—we must know more."

"Do you know nothing of them, then?" questioned the sister, opening her mild blue eyes a little wider as this new and startling fact presented itself.

"Well, it is this. Of course when she first became ill—before you came—I examined her things, and took away all money, and jewelry, and any letters I could find. That I was bound to do, naturally, in my own interest," he added, seeing that the nun looked somewhat startled at his announcement; "I was obliged to see that there was some money forthcoming for the expenses."

"Oh, yes, certainly!" stammered poor Sister Gabrielle, as he paused and looked for approbation.

"Well, now, the money which I found has come to an end. I looked for my address, to which to write, among her papers, and found one only. I wrote, and here is the reply." He handed an open letter to the nun. It ran as follows:

"Mrs. Hillyard begs to acknowledge the receipt of Monsieur Grosjean's communication with respect to Miss Falconer. She encloses a post-office order for ten pounds towards the expenses which M. Grosjean may have incurred and at the same time wishes to state that no further application will be entertained. Any letters from Miss Falconer, or from others on her behalf, will remain unanswered."

"*Voilà!*" commented the proprietor, as Sister Gabrielle folded and handed him back the letter. "No further hope in that quarter, you see."

"And is that the only address you have been able to find?"

"Absolutely the only one. Now, you see, this money will carry us on for a few days—my own expenses, I mean, nothing more; and for you, *ma sœur*, there is nothing; I wish to point it out to you."

"That does not matter; we are never paid. I mean we make no fixed charge; all whom we nurse, rich or poor, are expected to make some offering to the convent, according to their means, and the offerings of the rich pay for the expenses of attending on the poor."

Still, as Sister Gabrielle so bravely explained this, there was fading from her mind a hopeful little vision which she had been entertaining all this time, of her own triumphant return to the convent home bearing a substantial "offering" from the inmate of one of the biggest and grandest hotels in the Riviera.

"Well, we must await the course of events," sighed M. Grosjean in a dissatisfied fashion. "If the lady dies, which would be the simplest solution of the difficulty, I shall bury her with this"— waving the ten-pound note in his hand—"*et tout sera dit.* If she lives—*hélas!* there will be a long convalescence."

"Does not the consul sometimes help in these cases?" suggested the nun.

"If she were well, he could have her conveyed back to England—as a pauper; I do not know of anything else that he can do. However, I will see. Meanwhile please see if you can find any letters or papers among her things which may give us some clue to her friends. *Bon jour, ma sœur.*"

Sister Gabrielle went back to the little north room *au troisième* with a sad heart; and as she approached the bed to administer some nourishment at the appointed hour a thrill of pity and compassion came to her as she passed her hand under the hot, restless head, and held a spoon to the parched lips.

"Poor thing! poor thing!" she whispered to herself. "Homeless and friendless—I wonder why?"

As if the words had touched some chord in the sufferer's mind, she began to murmur some words, more connectedly than any the nun had heard hitherto. "Why? Why? Who knows why? Was it my system? It is a good one, yes! Yet listen: *Rouge perd—perd encore—toujours le rouge qui perd*—and those others, they win, and they do not need it as I do. . . . Which do you say is the lucky man? . . . I will ask—him—to give me a number—a number——" and her voice trailed away again into silence.

"I suppose she has been to that dreadful

Casino," innocently thought the nun. "Will she die, I wonder? Perhaps I ought to say something to her about it, if a gleam of consciousness comes. It is useless to send for a priest, as, no doubt, she is a Protestant. Is she, though? Well, if she were a Catholic there would surely be something to show it—some medal, scapular—something."

So, seeing that her patient had lapsed into quietude, she set to work to empty the big trunk which, with innate delicacy, she had hitherto refrained from touching, though *M. le Propriétaire's* rough hands had already tossed and tumbled about its contents. Now, knowing that for its owner's sake it was incumbent on her to seek information, she carefully examined every corner. Dress pockets, the little work-case, an empty card-case, two or three French novels of the usual yellow-covered kind, some torn sheets of paper dotted over with figures, the meaning of which Sister Gabrielle did not fathom, and vaguely supposed them to be "accounts," old concert programmes—was there nothing of the past among all these tumbled heaps of fine linen and lace, gloves and wraps, mostly old and worn, but still dainty in texture; no scrap of identity to be found anywhere?

As she pondered and puzzled over this strange absence of any clue to the sick's woman's identity, which she began to think must be intentional, the feeble voice began again its monotonous, broken words.

"It is only life that can fear dying. Possible loss means possible gain—gain? I never gain—it is all loss, loss, loss!"

"Could I not reach that bewildered brain?" thought Sister Gabrielle, rising from her kneeling position beside the trunk and going over to the bed. She took in her hands the crucifix which hung at her side and pressed it to the parched lips of the sufferer, whispering in low tones the word "Jesus." To her surprise the touch of the crucifix seemed to come to those babbling lips as a familiar thing, or perchance an awakening memory; the fevered hand clasped it round, and the murmuring voice began anew: "Sacred Heart—Heart of Jesus—mercy!"

"She is a Catholic!" said Sister Gabrielle to herself, speaking aloud in her astonishment. "No one but a Catholic would say that. And yet no scapular, no medal, no slightest token of religion anywhere. Poor soul! I fear she has forgotten God."

Presently she gave food again, and noticed afterwards that the patient seemed falling into a stupor.

"Yes," said the doctor, who came in shortly afterwards; "it is the crisis. If she awake from this stupor she will be saved."

"Otherwise she will pass away in it?"

"Probably." And he nodded farewell with a cheery air, as if to say that their watching would shortly be over.

Sister Gabrielle sat down beside the bed with an anxious heart; doubly so now that she guessed, or fancied, that a soul was there before her which, with all its sins upon it, was standing very near to the threshold of eternity. She took up her rosary and half mechanically began to say it, watching the while with eager eyes lest any change should come. But hours passed on, and the long night; and it was not until the morning sun was pouring its full flood of radiance through the unshaded pane that the sick woman opened her large, languid eyes wearily, but with full, tired consciousness, upon her watcher, and whispered faintly, "Who are you?"

CHAPTER III.

So the crisis had passed and she was saved!

Many a better life, to all human seeming, cherished and watched with passionate devotion, might have failed to struggle through the hour of trial; but this woman, whom apparently no one wanted, with no place in life as it seemed, no means even of subsistence, had retained her hold on life and was now slowly but surely coming back to strength, and—to what? Was it, as Sister Gabrielle thought to herself, as she watched her patient, lying propped up by pillows, with sad and troubled eyes turned towards the window, hardly speaking save to utter a brief word of thanks from time to time for services rendered; was it for the "one more grace" so often given that she had been thus brought back from the very gates of death?

One often wonders, watching beside a sick-bed or mourning some irreparable loss, why, where "one is taken and the other left," an Infinite Wisdom seems to choose those whom human love and human needs most cling to, rather than those who, like the sad-faced patient, seem of little use. Perhaps, like the subject of that unconsciously bitter remark which haunts one in its very simplicity of truth, they have "outlived their usefulness;" as was said of some old woman, a mother who had toiled all her life out for children and home, and now was no longer wanted there—"because, ma'am," said one for whom she had spent herself in youth, "she is of no more use—she has *outlived her usefulness!*"

"You will soon be able to get up now," said Sister Gabrielle encouragingly, as she took from the patient's hands an empty cup and lowered her pillow.

"Yes?" was the listless answer.

"Do you not care to recover?"

"Why should I?" And the dark eyes were turned on hers with an unutterable look of hopelessness in their depths.

The sister laid one hand upon the thin, trembling one before her, as she said, half-shyly, half-gravely, but very earnestly: "Do you not remember that

God has been very, very good to you in letting you live?"

"Would He not have been better to me in letting me die?" returned the other bitterly.

"Were you so ready to die then?" questioned the nun, half-fearing her own temerity, yet longing to speak the words that had been trembling on her lips for days. "You are a Catholic—I know you are——"

"How did you guess it?" broke in the other sharply.

"You told me yourself, without intending it, in your delirium."

"Ah! that's true—that wretched fever; tell me, did I say anything more—anything about my past, about myself?"

Sister Gabrielle shook her head.

"Nothing that I could understand. But what has been troubling me was—was—the thought that you might die unprepared."

"Has it? You poor, good little nun!" And the dark eyes softened for a moment as they turned an amused, half-sarcastic glance upon her. "You have been thinking of my poor soul, have you? Don't—it is not worth it!"

"Oh! do not say that: do not speak so. What would have become of you if you had died?"

The sick woman turned upon her pillow to look full into Sister Gabrielle's face.

"You remind me of a little pious story I once

heard—I wonder whether you know it? Listen. Give me that glass of water at your side. A girl who was—well, not a very good girl—was dying, and the friends round her bed spoke to her—well—as you want to talk to me. One of them asked her '*where she thought she was going?*' She dipped her finger in some water, like this"—she touched the water with her own—" and held it up before them all, one sparkling drop hanging on its tip. 'I am going,' she said, 'where I shall call in vain for one drop of water to cool my burning tongue.' And as she spoke the words she fell back and died!"

Sister Gabrielle could not repress a shudder at the picture thus set before her; but she quickly turned the subject by fetching from a table near a cup of beef-tea which had been warmed over her little spirit-lamp, and which was gratefully, even eagerly, consumed by the patient.

That evening she was again summoned to M. Grosjean's bureau.

"So it seems that your patient is recovering?" was his greeting to her.

"She has passed the crisis, yes, monsieur."

"Does she talk? Does she tell you anything about herself? You should encourage her to do so. And look here, *ma sœur*, I must ask you to speak to her about money matters now—my payment; it is time that she should write to her friends, if she has any, for I need not tell you that ten pounds has very nearly come to an end, even in hotel expenses; and how the doctor will be paid, I know not."

Poor Sister Gabrielle! She felt that she had never in all her life, even through the hardships of her two years' novitiate, had so painful a task to perform as on the following morning, when she essayed to convey the message of M. Grosjean to her patient. Yet she had but few words to say. "I understand," was her listener's calm comment, as she strove to convey, as delicately as possible, the proprietor's demand. "He wants to be paid—naturally. And I—I have nothing to pay him with. He has already taken all that was here, you say?"

"Everything of value except your watch; that is here," answered Sister Gabrielle, lifting it from the mantel-piece as she spoke.

"Ah, that is well! Give it to me here, please. I may need it yet." And she hid it carefully beneath her pillow, and lay back, evidently thinking painfully, for some time.

"Will you get me some paper, and a pen and ink, please?" she said at length with a visible effort. They were brought to her, and slowly, writing evidently with as much mental as bodily pain, she traced a few lines on two separate sheets of paper, and placed each in an envelope, which she addressed.

"Will you ask the proprietor to stamp these and send them?" she asked.

"I will go down with them myself," said the nun, glad to show that her mission had been so far successful. And she ran lightly down the three long flights of stairs to the tiny bureau where M. Grosjean sat all day long, like a merry spider in the centre of his web.

"What do you think now?" he exclaimed as he saw her; "that unfortunate patient of yours is destined to bring me nothing but misfortune. Her opposite neighbor has caught the fever!"

"Dear me, that is dreadful!" agreed the nun.

"I think the doctor wishes to ask you to undertake the case," went on M. Grosjean; "you see it is very difficult to find a nurse now; there is so much illness about that they are all engaged."

"My present patient is hardly well enough to be left yet," objected Sister Gabrielle.

"She will have to be left, however," retorted the proprietor, "for I do not intend to support a nurse for her any longer. It is hard enough for me to have to keep her—which, of course, I shall only do until she is well enough to leave."

Sister Gabrielle felt somewhat bewildered and shocked at this new turn that things were taking. She had not realized before that her very presence there was, in the eyes of the proprietor, an extra and uncalled-for expense, added to the burden which poor Miss Falconer was already felt to be. As she was extremely anxious to remain near her lonely patient, she began to review the circumstances in her mind, and to wonder whether she might venture to undertake a second case which, being so near her former patient, would enable her to give an occasional helping hand or word of comfort to the silent, lonely woman, about whom there hung an air of mystery and sorrow.

"Who is the new sufferer?" asked she, after a pause.

"A young gentleman who, with his bride, is here on their wedding tour," was the reply. "The lady is not strong enough to nurse him alone, and the present epidemic of influenza has taken away all the nurses. I should be very glad if you would stay, since you are already familiar with the situation, and do not fear infection."

So the end of it was that Sister Gabrielle found herself transferred to the opposite room—a large, sunny south one, under strict injunctions not to divulge the nature of the illness which she had lately tended, as well as to take every precaution to isolate and disinfect the sick-room. Her patient, a tall, fair young man, of some five-and-twenty years, seemed much less seriously affected than was the case with Miss Falconer, and had the advantage of every appliance and comfort that money—and the drugs from a fashionable English pharmacy—could bestow. The room was shut in by carbolized sheets; one leading to the corridor, and one to the bedroom adjoining where his young wife remained,

Sister Gabrielle whispering bulletins from time to time of his progress.

Every morning about nine o'clock—before entering upon his usual round of visits—the doctor, one of the fashionable English physicians of the place, would make his appearance by the bedside, and, cautiously pulling up his sleeve, touch with two timid fingers the sick man's pulse.

"Fever slackening? Ah, yes! That is right! Tongue, please?" and tiptoeing as far as possible from the reach of infected breath, he would cast a hasty glance at that member.

"Now, nurse, the carbolic!" And a vigorous application of carbolic soap to his hands would follow before with nervous haste he nodded farewell to his patient, and retired outside to continue his directions in the corridor. "Open the window, please, there! Ah! everything is going on well, I think, nurse?"

"Quite well, yes."

"We can do no better than continue present treatment—er—trust to nature to—er—restore vitality. (I beg your pardon, nurse, but will you keep on the *other* side of the current of air, letting it pass *from* me to you, do you see?")

"You are rather nervous about infection, I think?" remarked Sister Gabrielle one day, tired of his endless fidgety precautions.

"Well, you see"—he was a pompous little man

and talked in a consequential tone very irritating to the bystander—" I must consider my other patients. I have important cases on hand—most important. I am at present attending the Duchess of Oxford's little boy with measles, and it is a responsible position—most responsible!"

"But your passing through the fresh air carries off any harmful possibilities, surely?" urged she.

"Ah! infection is a subtle thing," he rejoined, dolefully shaking his head. "One may catch disease anywhere—cabs, railway carriages, narrow streets—all these are so many traps for the unwary. I assure you, nurse, when my wife and I go to England from here we carefully abstain as far as possible from touching the sides of the railway carriage, and never, never lean back in it! There is nothing more you would wish to ask with reference to the patient, is there?"

This was a delicate hint, repeated each morning, intended to convey the fact that the good man was ready for his fee, which, to avoid any misunderstanding, he preferred to pocket at the close of each visit; and accordingly Sister Gabrielle would disappear for a moment into the adjoining room, and come out with the regulation twenty-franc piece in her hand.

"Good morning!" And Sister Gabrielle would retire behind her protecting sheet, and nurse her patient by the light of her own judgment for the next twenty-four hours.

Sometimes, when he was asleep and she knew that she could leave him safely, she would go quietly out, and steal into the dull little back room where Marion Falconer sat day after day in a broken arm-chair, essaying her strength by pacing slowly and painfully from chair to bed and bed to window, gazing out with large and melancholy eyes upon the changeful hues of the mountain beyond and the cleft valley, whence a snow-swollen rivulet trickled downwards to the sea; the only breaks in the monotony of these long, dreary hours being the infrequent trays of comfortless meals, thrust into the doorway by a hasty hand, and a few moments' chat with her former nurse. The doctor had ceased his visits, having pronounced her out of danger, and, perchance, perceiving small chance of obtaining his fee. Every day when Sister Gabrielle entered she would turn her wistful looks towards the doorway, with " Are the letters come, do you know? No letter for me, sister?"

And Sister Gabrielle would shake her head, with some hopeful word which indeed she hardly felt. But the silent, almost awful reserve which encased the sick woman was a barrier which few, and certainly not that timid little nun, could break through. She would hover round her wistfully, and glance at her with shy, appealing looks as she talked in broken sentences of unimportant matters, longing all the time to speak to her of what in very truth she was *waiting to say*—but waiting in vain.

"Is there any English confessor here, I wonder?" she suggested one day as an opening for conversation. "Or perhaps you go to confession in French?"

"Or perhaps not at all?" suggested her questioner, with a faintly ironical smile.

"Would you not like to see a priest, after—having been in such danger of death?"

"I? Oh, no, not at all. Besides, I thought the danger was past?"

"The more reason you have for gratitude," returned Sister Gabrielle quickly, glad even of this slight opening for speaking out her heart.

"This is a great deal to be grateful for, is it not?" spoke Marion Falconer, with a quick little sweep of her hand round the bare room.

"Life *is* a great thing to be grateful for," she answered, "and the future lies in your own power."

"The future?" For once Miss Falconer's indifferent reserve seemed broken through, as she rose and paced with weak, uncertain steps about the room. "What is my future, do you think? Oh, you poor little innocent, ignorant soul! do you know what my life is—what my future is? Look at me! Have I a friend in the world? Is there one single hand that I can grasp or cling to for help, in all the universe? Have I an acquaintance even who would not, if they heard of my death to-night, say, 'What a mercy that she is gone'? Look! I am waiting—waiting in a sick despair—

to answers to my last appeals for help; and they will not come—I know that! And by-and-by, when I am a little stronger, or the landlord is a little more tired of waiting for the money that never comes, I shall be politely told to go, and leave my worldly goods behind me—such as they are," she added with a dreary little laugh ; " and then—when I walk away from this door—what do you propose that I should do then ? "

Sister Gabrielle was silent.

" What is left to me but to do what the fever failed to do ? I am thinking over it, every day as I sit here, trying to decide how it is to be. Will it be poison ? That is very painful—and besides, I shall have no hole of shelter to crawl into to die; one can't die out in the open street. Will it be the sea? I don't like the sea; it is shallow and difficult to reach, and one is ignominiously rescued. I am not a man, and I have not the stereotyped revolver of Monte Carlo usage; so——"

" Oh, please ! " gasped Sister Gabrielle, " don't talk like that. I know you don't mean it, but——"

" Not mean it ? " returned the other with a grim little smile, which somehow carried conviction with it. " Well, I hope the proprietor will ' not mean it ' when he turns me out into the streets, in a day or two. Perhaps you will kindly make that remark to him ? "

Sister Gabrielle stood dumbly looking at her for a moment, feeling as if no words were adequate to touch that profound despair. Suddenly her hand, moving mechanically downwards, encountered the rosary at her side, and with an impulsive movement she unfastened and laid it upon Miss Falconer's lap; then, putting both arms round her neck, she kissed the unresponsive cheek; and turning, hurried from the room.

CHAPTER IV.

In very truth Sister Gabrielle did not in the least guess at her former patient's past or even present life. The ravings of fever, the pencil notes and jottings lying here and there, every indication which would have enlightened a more " worldly " person, passed by her unnoticed and uncomprehended. All that she did take in, however, of the poor wanderer's pitiful and solitary state made her yearn, with the tenderness of a true womanly soul, over that forlorn one to whom by some mysterious overruling of Divine Mercy she had been brought to minister. In after years she used to say that she had never realized until then the terrible inequality of rich and poor against which so many thousands have impotently and wrongly rebelled. In one room sunshine, and comfort, and love—all combining to make human suffering light —in the other poverty, want, despair; within a stone's throw, each to each. And in both rooms the same great, underlying need which, if supplied, would have enriched and ennobled both—the same lack of faith and God.

The mission of those who have devoted their lives to the service of the sick and dying is, without doubt, primarily the healing of the body; but there is surely with them also an underlying apostolate of ministration to souls. Among the poor this work is ostensible, almost easy, we would say. With patients of the upper class it is hardly less needful, and requires far more tact, delicacy, and courage for its exercise. If all were known, there have been not a few conversions from heresy as well as those from indifference and sin, wrought by the ministrations of a " nursing sister;" and even those who seem to reap but little benefit from the spiritual side of their ministration, are loud in praise of its temporal advantages.

The second patient whom Sister Gabrielle had been called to tend was a big, light-hearted, muscular young Englishman who, when his time of convalescence began, seemed to live in a perpetual state of half-amused annoyance at the untoward illness which, for the first time in his cheery, irresponsible life, had come upon him. " Queer, isn't it ? to feel so weak," he would ejaculate, lifting a feeble hand and arm into the air and pinching its softened muscles amazedly. " How much longer is this sort of thing going to last ? "

" Oh ! you will soon be sitting up by the fire if

you go on as you are doing," the sister would assure him.

"Yes, and then begin to crawl out-of-doors, wrapped up in shawls, like all the rest of the poor creatures Minnie and I used to laugh at!" he continued. "The idea of my being laid by the heels in this wretched place, where three-quarters of the people are consumptives, and the fourth Monte Carloites!"

"What, do you mean gamblers?" ejaculated Sister Gabrielle with awe. "Are there any of *those* here? Not in this hotel, surely?"

"Well—I should think you might tell that better than most!"

"I?"

"Considering that you have been nursing one of them—have you not?"

"You don't mean——" and then all at once a light broke upon her bewildered brain, and she understood the meaning of her perplexities.

"That lady opposite, whom you nursed; she is one of the regular old stagers—frequenters of 'the tables,' you know."

"I did not know it. How did you?"

"They told me down-stairs—the landlord, I think. I declare I should like to make her acquaintance, and get her to teach me the ins and outs of these wonderful 'systems' they talk so much about. Don't seem to have done much for her, though, do they? I heard she was just about cleaned out!"

"I'm afraid she is," answered Sister Gabrielle gravely. And her thoughts went off again to the problem which was exercising them night and day; how to help that soul which lay at her door, as it were, in sore need of rescue.

"Can you spare me for half an hour, do you think, to go into the town?" she asked of her patient.

"Oh, dear, yes! by all means, nurse. And you might get me some papers at the same time."

So she hurried off; for a thought had come to her of the way to continue her apostolate of souls. Her destination was a well-stocked "*librairie,*" or book-shop, which she had noticed once before, as announcing itself to speak English and provide the newest English books.

"Do you sell rosaries?" she asked them; but they only stared in perplexity, and showed her a variety of objects, from penholders to artificial flowers.

"Rosaries—'chaplets,'" she insisted, and could not show them her own, because she had left it on Marion Falconer's lap.

"*Madame demande un chaplet,*" explained the shop-boy, retiring to giggle with his confrère at the back of the counter.

"No, we do not sell '*des objets religieux,*'" explained the master, coming forward.

"Where can I find some?"

"*Ma foi! je ne sais pas.* Perhaps up in the old town—not here."

No, not there. Not where *the English church*, with its parsonage and garden; English-speaking shops which 'closed on Sundays,' and held notices of every variety of Protestant service; where the English influence and English religion were paramount, and Catholicism a thing of the people, a superstition of the aborigines, to be sneered at like Hinduism in India, and its attributes kept well out of sight.

So she left the fashionable quarter—the Mentone as it is known to the world of to-day—and toiled up a steep litle dingy street to the vicinity of the parish church, where, after some difficulty, in an odd little shop, which sold wools and gloves and a few fly-blown old religious pictures, she succeeded in finding the object of her search.

"I am later out than I expected to be," she explained as she made her reappearance, rather breathless and tired, in her patient's room. "I could not find what I wanted except in the old town. And now, when I have made you comfortable, may I leave you again for a few minutes?"

And soon she was knocking at the door of Miss Falconer's room.

By this time, it should be said, Marion Falconer had sufficiently recovered strength to be able to put on her walking things each morning, and creep slowly down-stairs and out into the bright, warm sunshine. Sister Gabrielle had managed to disinfect her room, and she was only deterred from taking her place with the rest of the world downstairs by the dread of receiving her sentence of dismissal from the landlord. So that on this still, warm and sunny afternoon Sister Gabrielle was not surprised to find her standing before the tall gilt mirror over the mantel-piece arranging her bonnet and veil to go out.

"I have come to redeem my rosary—by bringing you another," said the nun, smiling brightly as she entered; "you will not mind my giving you one, will you? For as I have not seen one among your possessions I fancy you must have lost yours."

"I have indeed lost it—many years since," replied Miss Falconer, with a wan little smile, as she turned from the glass and took the sister's two outstretched hands in hers with a sort of grave tenderness with which she now always received her. "You are very good to think of it—and of me, as you do."

"It is a poor, commonplace little one," said the former speaker; "only for your use until you have a better one." And she placed a small red rosary in the other's palm.

"*Red! Rouge gagne!*" exclaimed Miss Falconer, almost gayly, as she took it. "Is it an omen—may I take it so, I wonder?" Then, seeing the shocked look on Sister Gabrielle's face: "Oh!

I horrify you, I know, dear sister. I cannot help it; all my thoughts turn one way! Will it please you better if I tell you that I actually used your rosary last night?"

"Yes indeed, I *am* glad. But do not let me keep you now; you are going out."

A shade fell over the transient brightness of Marion Falconer's face as these words recalled her to herself. "Yes, I am going out," she said, "and you will not like to hear where!"

"Tell me."

"In the first place, the sentence has been pronounced; the landlord informed me this morning that I must leave to-morrow."

"Oh!" gasped Sister Gabrielle, "what will you do?"

"I am going to try one last chance—one last throw for fortune."

"What do you mean?"

"Listen. I pawned my watch this morning, and got this for it," showing some gold-pieces in her worn, shabby purse. "With this I am going, *for the last time*, to Monte Carlo."

"Oh, *don't!*" broke in her listener.

"I shall stake it all—in a way that will double, treble itself, if it wins; and if I win I promise you I will play no more; yes, I know that is what you are asking me. I shall have enough then to support myself for a few days while gaining more strength to seek employment.

"And if you lose?"

"Then—don't ask!" she answered abruptly.

"But—but why not live for those few days on what you have there?"

"Because I must, must, *must* have one throw more! I cannot help it, the madness of it is upon me; you cannot understand the irresistibleness of the temptation."

"I am afraid you are resisting grace," said Sister Gabrielle sadly.

"Don't say that, but wish me good luck! There! Good-by—and—and—pray for me!" She bent down and kissed the cheek of her new-found friend, and taking up the long-handled sunshade, with which she supported her still somewhat uncertain footsteps, she quitted the room. Sister Gabrielle took up her own large rosary, which lay upon the table near, and knelt down to say a portion of it "for that soul which is in danger of losing grace," as she whispered, before she left, with slow and saddened steps, that dull and cheerless room.

CHAPTER V.

IT was somewhat early on the following morning—perhaps about eight o'clock or so—that Sister Gabrielle, coming for a moment out into the corridor into which all the rooms opened, found herself face to face with, almost knocking against, in fact, a little group of men who were entering the room in front of her, No. 27. "Why, that is Miss Falconer's room," she thought; "surely that unfeeling landlord has not turned her out already!"

In another moment the identical individual himself appeared, his usually smiling appearance having given place to one of grave concern; and, without noticing the looker-on, he passed her and went after the others into the room. A vague feeling of uneasy surprise drew Sister Gabrielle to linger just within the doorway of the room she had quitted and now re-entered, with some faint idea of catching and interpellating the landlord at his exit. Presently they came out, talking low, and still not observing her; and she heard M. Grosjean address the foremost gentleman, a quiet-looking, elderly Englishman, as "Monsieur le Consul." Presently, much to her surprise, she saw them close and lock the door, and a young man, who acted as the consul's aide or secretary, proceeded to affix seals to it in a very business-like manner, while his superior slowly paced up and down the corridor conversing in a low voice with the landlord. When the official seals were duly affixed they departed, and silence again reigned throughout the place.

Sister Gabrielle went back into the room and rang the bell once, twice, for the *femme de chambre;* then came outside to avoid speaking in the invalid's room.

"Did you ring for hot water? Here it is, *ma*

sœur!" said the lively chambermaid, whose services had considerably improved in attentiveness since Sister Gabrielle had begun to require them on behalf of a rich Englishman instead of a lonely and impecunious " demoiselle."

"What does that mean?" whispered the nun, pointing to the sealed-up door.

"Ah, yes! It is dreadful, is it not?"

"I do not know; what is it? What has happened?" almost gasped her listener.

"*Quoi, vous ne savez pas?* She is dead, that lady who was there."

"*Dead?*"

The girl nodded. "Some accident, I do not know what it was rightly. Some say, indeed, that she destroyed herself. Anyhow she was to have left to-day, and now—*voilà!* Are you ready for the coffee yet?"

"Yes—no—I mean yes, bring it," said Sister Gabrielle confusedly, her eyes still fixed upon the two great splotches of red wax, stamped with the English arms, which seemed to grow larger and larger before her eyes. And then she had to control herself and go in and attend upon her invalid, who was very vivacious, and talked of going for a drive, and getting disinfected, and casting aside this horrid old fever. And then, for the first time, she found herself hailing with positive pleasure the doctor's well-known tap at the door, listened patiently to the scraps of chat and questions of news with which the patient plied him, as the only representative of the outside world whom he could at present reach, and followed him as sedately, to all outward appearance, from the room as on any other ocasion.

Ah!" he exclaimed, as on closing the door behind him he caught sight of the red seals opposite, "that is the room, is it? Sad business, eh?"

"Tell me what it is, please; I do not quite understand what has happened. Have you heard it all?"

"Just met the consul as I was coming up here, and he told me. Some lady, one of those regular Monte Carlo people who come to stay here and go up every day to 'the tables.'"

"To—to gamble, you mean?"

"Yes, yes, *roulette* and *rouge et noir*, and so forth, you know. The sort of people who go in for it as a profession, a means of livelihood, you know."

"Yes—well?"

"Well, this person it appears used to go up there every day (only she had been ill lately and had not gone), and yesterday evening, as she was returning home, on arriving at the station and alighting from the train she—well they don't know whether accidentally or on purpose, but at all events she got entangled as the train was moving on—and killed."

An exclamation of horror broke, involuntarily, from the lips of the nun. The doctor suddenly turned and faced her.

"Why—why—wasn't that the very woman you were nursing before you took my patient—the first case, from whom he was supposed to have caught the fever?"

She nodded, unable for a moment to speak.

"Then, bless my soul! you'll be wanted at the inquest most likely. They are trying in vain to find out anything about her—who she was—her relatives, friends, anything. I must remind the consul!"

"Oh, pray, pray, don't!" breathed the nun, to whom the word "inquest" meant unutterable horrors.

"But you must, you know!" he persisted. "I suppose you know all about her?"

"Indeed I know nothing, nothing. Ask the landlord if I am not fully as ignorant as himself."

"Oh! well, excuse me, but that's not possible. You who were with her, night and day, for weeks—at all events, I shall tell the consul!" And, full of importance, he hurried away down the stairs, and she heard his footsteps die away in the distance.

An hour or two passed, and she went about her work as usual, with a sickening horror at her heart and a dreary longing to hear more of the tragedy which lay, as it were, at their door. Then a tap and a whispered summons came, and she found herself standing before M. Grosjean beside the still sealed door.

"You know what has happened?" he said to her very gravely. "Can you tell us anything about—her; anything which may be of use at the inquest?"

She shook her head. "You know that I never heard anything of her past or of her friends; you asked me that before."

"When did you see her last?"

"Yesterday."

"Morning or afternoon?"

"Afternoon. I went in to see her, and found her dressed to go out. She went while I was there."

"So you were almost the last person to speak to her, hereabouts at least. Well, how did she seem?"

"Much as usual. Perhaps rather brighter than usual."

"Did she tell you that I had given her notice to leave?"

"Yes."

"What did she say about it?"

"She said that she was going to 'try her luck' once more."

"And did she say what she would do if she lost?"

"No." Thankful indeed was Sister Gabrielle to be able to speak that "no." She knew what was the underlying thought in the questioner's mind, the scarcely defined dread in her own; and there rose up in her mind a wild desire to combat that suspicion.

"Well, you can tell me nothing more?" questioned M. Grosjean. "It is very perplexing. One does not know what to do. The consul has telegraphed to the lady who wrote once before—you remember? The only address we have."

"You—they will not want to question me—elsewhere, will they?"

"Oh, I suppose not, unless the consul wishes to see you."

"Do tell me, please"—she hesitated as to how to word her inquiry—"how do they think it happened?"

"They say that either she missed her footing and fell under the carriage, or——" he shrugged his shoulders with a significant gesture.

"She fell down, I am sure of it!" responded the nun eagerly; "you know she was still very, very weak from her illness; I have often seen her stumble in going up-stairs.

"Ha! yes, that is true. I must tell them that! You see, it is very disagreeable for me; people saying that she was in despair—that—that I was hard upon her, in fact. I do not think so; do you? I really could not keep her forever."

"No." said his hearer mechanically; and within herself she was thinking, "one cannot expect a hotel-keeper to be merciful; but what an awful,

awful thing it would be to drive a fellow-creature to despair!"

"Monsieur Grosjean," she called softly after him as he was turning away, "one thing I should like to ask you."

"À votre service, ma sœur?"

"Where is—*she*?"

"The body, you mean? In a room near the station. It will be buried to-morrow."

"I should like to see her once more. Would it be possible?"

"Why—yes, I suppose so. I will write a line which you can present to the people of the house, and they will admit you. Come to my bureau down-stairs when you want it."

"Thank you."

She went in to her patient, who was tranquilly unconscious of the tragedy, and told him she was going out. Then, exchanging her indoor for an outdoor veil, she set forth duly furnished with an order for admittance from the landlord. It was a lovely morning, the sunlight sparkling on a thousand ripples over the sea, the clear blue headlands standing out distinct and fair along the coast, Bordighera and San Remo and all the Italian coast on the one hand, and on the other the white gleam of fair, foul, Circe-like Monte Carlo, like some vile, beauteous traitress, laughing beneath the warmth of the sun.

"What a beautiful world God has made, and

how man has destroyed it!" she thought to herself, as we all have thought when we gaze on the loveliness of earth and sea and sky which men call "the Riviera." Even Sister Gabrielle—though she was a somewhat prosaic little soul—felt uplifted for a moment into a feeling of that delight in living, that contentment in the mere sense of existence, which so seldom visits the inhabitants of any duller clime, and which one pictures to one's self as the true keynote of human joy in the old Greek times. And this all-pervading beauty and entrancement of nature in early summer helped to bring a sharp, painful shock to her mind as she crossed the threshold of the darkened house indicated in her paper of directions, and knew herself in the presence of death.

"You know the *povera donna?*" questioned the gaunt, black-haired woman who guarded the deathchamber, and reached down with one hand a key from the wall above her, while the other arm supported a little swarthy "*bambino*" swaddled in rags.

"Yes, I knew her," answered the nun, gathering, though imperfectly, the sense of the *patois* speech.

The woman turned the key and signed to her to enter the room beyond, where, on a humble bed, lay a shrouded form. Yes, it was Marion Falconer. The sad, dark eyes which she had watched so often turning in hopeless longing towards the light were closed now, in everlasting rest. The poor, thin hands were folded peacefully upon her breast, and as Sister Gabrielle laid her own warm one upon them she started, for there beneath her touch, twined tightly among the stiff fingers, was the little red rosary she had given.

"Yes," nodded the woman, noticing her start of surprise, "it is a chaplet. It was found clasped in her hands when she died, and I placed it there. One would have thought she had been a Catholic, would not one? Only it is not so, of course, for she was an *Inglese*, and they are not *Cristiani*."

"She *was* a Catholic," answered the nun, in her broken Italian. "You must tell them so." And then she knelt and prayed, with a strange, dream-like sense of sorrow and loss for the soul whose earthly tenement she had so long tended, until the woman grew impatient at her stay, and she knew she must return to her own work. "*You* will no more come back to that dull room, to sadness and pain, and weary waiting and anxious fears," she whispered, leaning over the quiet dead form. "Do you know now how I prayed for you? I will still pray, all my life, for your soul; and—*God is very merciful*. Good-by, dear; good-by!" And she kissed the white, cold lips, and went back into the southern sunshine.

* * * * *

And this was all—all that Sister Gabrielle ever knew; for one's prayers are not always visibly answered in this world. And so it was that the tender-hearted little nun had never the consolation of learning (until, perchance, it was told her by angel voices in the hereafter) how the trembling footsteps *had*, even as she hoped, turned backwards like those of the Prodigal, to " arise and go to the Father," with a last plaintive appeal to Mary on her lips and in her heart as she clasped the little rosary, when the Divine Mercy, more merciful than its creatures, answered that appeal by a brief and all but painless death.

KATHARINE TYNAN HINKSON.

Miss Katharine Tynan was born in Dublin, and educated at the Dominican Convent of St. Catharine of Siena, in Drogheda. She began to write verse when very young, and her first poem appeared in *The Graphic*. In 1885 was published her first book, " Louise de la Vallière and Other Poems." It was a success and quickly ran into several editions. This book was followed by " Shamrocks," in 1887, and " Ballads and Lyrics " in 1892. Her first prose work was " The Life of Mother M. Xaveria Fallon," which also appeared in 1892. Since then she has published " A Cluster of Nuts," being sketches of Irish life ; " Cuckoo Songs,"

"The Way of a Maid," "The Land of Mist and Mountain," "Miracle Plays," "An Isle in the Water," and "Oh, What a Plague is Love!"

A critic says of her: "All her poems are marked by delicacy and musical deftness; but in her stories she has shown a breadth of treatment, humor, and deep knowledge of human nature that are not evident in her poetical compositions to anything like the same extent." That her genius is remarkably versatile is shown by a comparison of "An Isle in the Water" and "Oh, What a Plague is Love!" The one is a collection of short stories depicting the loves, passions, and hatreds of the rude mountain and sea folk, and for its vigor has been likened to the plays of Ibsen and the novels of Toorgenef; the other deals with the frivolities and artificialities of fashionable life, and is equally as good in its way as the first.

Miss Tynan was married in 1893 to Mr. H. A. Hinkson, who is also engaged in literary work, and since her marriage she has made her home in the neighborhood of London. She is a constant contributor of stories, articles, and reviews to the literary magazines of England, and an occasional writer for *The Pilot* and *The Ave Maria* in the United States.

The Wardrobe.

BY KATHARINE TYNAN HINKSON.

"Well, then, John Marnane," said one of the neighbors, "an' what brings the like o' you here at all? Thinkin' o' furnishin', John, hey?"

John grinned all over his sunburnt face, uncouth in its stubby beard. Hay dust was powdered over his old coat and on his thick hair, hiding the places where it was fast turning gray. He was a grotesque figure, yet under his shaggy brows the blue eyes were mild and innocent, and as he drawled an answer his voice was gentle. At the sound of it his old pony, in a little chaise long innocent of the mop and bucket, lifted its head and whinnied.

"I came where I saw the crowd," John explained. "I thought there must be divarsion goin' on."

"Well, John," said the other, facetiously, "aren't you a great fellow all out for divarsion? Look here, boys," to a crowd of his friends, "here's John Marnane on the lookout for a wife. He's here to buy the furniture. Stand by me, John, an' I'll advise you."

The others gathered round to join in the joke, and for a few minutes the auctioneer paused with uplifted hammer, and smiled sympathetically. He, too, had known John Marnane from childhood, and enjoyed the friendly badgering he was taking so well. But business cannot long wait on pleasure. The languid bidding was for an old wardrobe, cumbrous and ugly, and as big as the side of a house.

"A pound for this beautiful article, a pound, going at a pound, a guinea, one pound half-a-crown, one pound five. Mr. Marnane, allow me to call your attention to this commodious article. It's dirt-cheap at the money. You couldn't make a handsomer present to the mistress to hang her dresses in. What did you say, Mr. Marnane? Twenty-seven shillings?"

He leaned over frolicsomely. The men at John's elbow grinned and encouraged him.

"Come on now, John. Be a man an' spake up. There isn't such a chance once in a lifetime."

"Sure you could get herself an' her gew-gaws and the girl's frocks an' the boys' shuits 'idin it. 'Tis as big as a Noah's Ark."

"The girls is watchin' you, John. Show them the spunk you've in you."

John, bashfully grinning, wriggled in the hands of his friendly tormentors. As he looked from side to side for a loophole of escape he caught sight of a pretty face dimpling all over with enjoyment of the joke. It was a rosy face, with little teeth between wide scarlet lips, and roguish eyes under upward-curling black lashes. Something went through John Marnane like an electric shock. For a second it seemed to himself as if he must have trembled in his captors' hands, then he was quiet again and looking carefully in the opposite direction.

"Now, Mr. Marnane, you've a bidder against you. Twenty-seven shillings! any advance on twenty-seven shillings? Did you speak, Miss?" to the pretty girl. "Are you hesitating, Mr. Marnane, an' the eyes of a purty girl leppin' out of her to be the mistress of the wardrobe?"

"Twenty-eight!" said John Marnane.

A roar of delight burst from the crowd.

"Twenty-eight shillings! Thank you, Mr. Marnane. Any bidding over twenty-eight? Twenty-eight shillings for a wardrobe as big as the *Great Aistern!* Twenty-eight shillings! Going, going, gone! The wardrobe to Mr. Marnane, Johnny."

The auctioneer's clerk made his entry broadly grinning. Every one was grinning except John himself, who had grown deadly serious. One article after another of Father Sheeran's heavy, old-fashioned furniture was put up. John kept bidding with steady determination.

The savor went out of the joke by degrees. They had thought they were egging on the man to acquire things he had no use for. Now, it would seem that he had come with the deliberate intention of purchasing. Curiosity took the place of laughter on the faces of the crowd: only a few irate matrons who had come bargain-hunting protested they needn't have come there at all, at all, if they had had word that Mr. Marnane wanted everything.

As John pushed his way out of the crowd after the auction was over, Larry Brophy, the man who had just accosted him, took him by the arm.

"Well, aren't you a sly fellow, John," he said seriously, "to do your coortin' on the quiet, unbeknownst to us all? She's not a girl from these parts, anyhow?"

John looked at him with the gambling excitement of the auction still in his eyes. He looked quite different somehow from the John Marnane whom it had seemed natural to ridicule earlier in the day. He had the air of a man with responsibilities. The slouch had disappeared from his gait, and he looked taller.

"No," he said, "you don't know her."

"Come up to my place and have a glass of grog, and tell us all about her. Were you courtin' her in the mother's lifetime? You must have been, you sly dog, for sure the poor ould woman's only six weeks, come Tuesday, in her grave."

John drew himself gently from the detaining hand. "I can't talk about it yet, Larry," he said with dignity, "and I can't come up to-night, thank you kindly, all the same. I've things to see to at my own place."

"Well, then, if you won't, you won't," said the other, a little offended. "Though how you can employ yourself of an evening in that ould place o' yours, wid not a sowl to spake to but ould Margaret Connors fairly bothers me."

John Marnane went on without a word. If the two men had been together a minute longer Brophy might have been enlightened. As John was mounting his shabby old car, a little ass-cart drove out before him into the road. The driver was the pretty girl with the pink cheeks. In the back of the cart she had a few common household utensils she had picked up cheaply. She wore a poor, little cotton frock of a pink color, out of which she looked like a moss rosebud. She sat on a plank crossing the cart, and jogged the ass along with a loose rein. At the sight of her something fierce and hungry leaped into John Marnane's quiet eyes. It was there for a second before it was replaced by the sleepy affectionateness, which was his normal expression like that of a well-treated dog. He waited a minute or two to let the girl go on. Then he followed, making his pony walk, while, with an elaborate pretence, he lighted his old clay pipe.

The girl took the road up the mountain. John followed, driving very slowly, and keeping her in sight. He was so engrossed in watching her that it never occurred to him what people might think if they met him on a road leading directly away from his home.

It was hawthorn time, and the dewy evening was full of fragrance. The wild roses were opening, and a few early meadows were cut. Still the corncrake was sawing monotonously, and the cuckoo was calling close at hand. A little crescent of a new moon in the sky had a faint silver star within its horns.

The girl pulled up at a little thatched cabin by the side of a boreen twisting up the mountain. As she stopped John pulled up his pony. He knew now where the girl lived, and was satisfied. He jogged homewards in the dewy twilight full of a sweet disturbance such as he had never known in all his fifty years. An unexpected fount of romance, a spring of boyishness in John Marnane's elderly heart had been tapped to-day.

He drove up to his house-front, suddenly aware of its deficiencies. It was a square, ugly house, such as they build in Ireland. Three windows above, two below, with a hall-door in the middle displayed their uninviting symmetry. The sloping roof was of blue slate; the hall-door had once been painted green, but the paint had come off in flakes, and the knocker was broken. The uncurtained windows were like black patches in the whitewashed walls. A broken barrow lay by the hall-door, half hidden among dock and dandelion. The gravel path was covered with coarse grass and rubbish of old iron and broken crockery. In what once had been a flower-bed there was a heap of dry dust: it was the dust-bath of the hens. John Marnane shook his grizzling head deprecatingly.

"It did me and the old woman, God rest her, well enough, but it won't do for her at all, at all."

He put up his pony leisurely, and went in. On the kitchen table a coarse cloth was flung, with a blue crockery mug, a black-handled knife and fork, some salt in an egg-cup, and a jug of buttermilk.

He glanced at these homely preparations for his supper, and around the smoke-browned kitchen in the bare rafters of which the hens were roosting. A handful of smouldering turf ashes was on the hearth, and from the hook in the black chimney there swung a pot of floury potatoes. There were tins on the wall and crockery on the tall dresser, but all were one color with the smoke. Old Peg sat on her heels by the turf embers cooking a rasher of coarse bacon, and a blear-eyed old dog wagged his tail feebly as John Marnane came in.

"You're late home," the old woman said querulously. "I hope you're not goin' to take to gad now herself is gone."

John Marnane looked at her as if he had not heard her. He went through the kitchen into a mean and dirty hall skirting a narrow staircase. He opened the door at the right-hand side and looked in. A musty smell came from the place, an odor of dampness mixed with the all-pervading turf-smoke. The tattered blinds were down, and he could not make out in the dark the round table, the green rep chairs and couch, the gilt looking-glass, and the colored religious pictures which were the adornments of the late Mrs. Marnane's best parlor. Still those glories were there hiding in the darkness. John Marnane smiled to himself. The best parlor was not to say a comfortable room, but with her in it things would be different. She was sure to be pleased with the furniture, and the Brussels carpet with roses, and the hearth-rug, and the shavings interspersed with silver and gold tinsel in the grate.

He opened the other door with less satisfaction. There were sacks of potatoes all round the wall, and the only articles of furniture were his mother's shiny old arm-chair and the tall, ungainly office desk, with its high stool, at which since his mother died he had laboriously pored over his accounts. He looked around the dusky room. He could have thought that he saw the old mother sitting there, erect in her rusty black, with the nodding purple ribbons and red flowers in her cap. He quailed at the thought. He had been dutifully fond of his mother, and had grieved for her with the forlornness of one from whom after half a century a fetter has been removed. But, good son as he was, he had never entered that room while she sat there without feeling like a truant schoolboy. Why, up to the last day she lived it had been a fiction between them that he had never learned to smoke.

He struck a match and lit the tallow candle that was stuck in a bottle on the desk.

"She was a great old woman," he said to himself, "an' did better by me thin I'd ever ha' done by myself. Still it might ha' been better if she'd given me more of a voice in things. I wouldn't be so terrible helpless an' good for nothin' now."

He went up-stairs, the candle guttering down the bottle on to his hands all the time. A grotesque shadow of himself went after him up the gaunt walls, where the gray plaster had grown grimy. On the landing he stepped into a hole in the floor. He shook his head gently.

"'Twould be a nasty place for a little, soft foot," he muttered. "I'll have in Flynn to see to it."

He went into one of the bedrooms. The tester bedstead, with its torn hangings, stood in the midst of what with its two windows might have been a pleasantly light and airy room. The bed was covered with a tattered patchwork quilt. The bare floor had the grime of ages upon it, and cobwebs hung from window to window. The unpapered walls were covered with stains, and in many places there was the smoke where a candle had been allowed to lean too near, or had toppled over in its primitive candlestick. A couple of cane-bottomed chairs had lost their seats. A painted deal dressing-table was covered with candle-grease and other dirt, and the glass upon it was green in color and cracked from end to end. John Marnane shook his head more violently than before.

He put down the candle on the chimney-piece, and his eyes half-closed, a trick he had acquired in his many moments of lonely reflection. He was remembering a bedroom he had once seen when he had visited a cousin. It had pink roses on a trellis for its wall-paper, and white lace curtains tied with pink bows, and a dressing-table draped with shiny pink calico and lace. He wondered whether he could imitate that delightful room. In a vision he saw this uninviting bed-chamber so transfigured.

As he turned away he caught sight of a distorted reflection of himself in the cracked looking-glass. For a second a horrible misgiving smote him. Then he deliberately turned the thing round. If he had been another kind of man he would probably have kicked it to pieces, for it had given him a horrible fright, and he had felt a quiver of that mingled rage and fear which is one of the most driving of passions. But as the glass turned away its cracked face he recovered himself with an awkward smile.

"It would make a show of a saint, so it would," he muttered. "I was the quare-lookin' *gom* with them cracks runnin' up an' down my cheeks, for all the world like ould swoord-cuts. For a minute it staggered me, till it came back upon me that it was th' ould cracks in the glass."

He shook off his fright as one might brush away a troublesome insect, and went down to the kitchen, where he sat cheerfully to his supper.

"Peg," he said, in the course of conversation, "did you ever hear my mother say rightly what age I was?"

"You'll be fifty come Michaelmas. You were born a week after my own Bat, Lord rest him."

"Would you say, Peggy," with an air of embarrassment, "that fifty was what you'd call gettin' on for a man?"

"*Gettin' on!* You'll be gettin' on whin you're seventy. What's puttin' such notions into your mind?"

"My mother trated me as a child, Peggy, an', upon my word, I often feel very young. She used to say that a man was a boy as long as he wasn't marrid."

"The world knows that. People's marryin' younger now—the men is, I mane. Why, I remember whin a man didn't get lookin' about him till he was gettin' on for sixty."

"I should be young o' my age, too. I never went drinkin', or card-playin', or to a wrastlin'-match, or a cock-fight. The mother wouldn't have it, as you know, Peg."

"She was right. They're dirty occupations."

"You don't think any one 'ud call me old, Peg?" he asked anxiously.

"What's come to the man? If it's match-making you're after, you're the match o' the youngest girl in the barony."

John Marnane drew a relieved sigh.

"You don't think the young girls falls in love wid their aiquils in age?"

"Falls in love! God forgive you, John Marnane, what would your poor mother say if she heard you? What nonsense is in your head? Girls don't fall in love, at laste if they're what they ought to be. They takes the boy their match is made with, an' thankful. I never knew but one case of what they called 'fallin' in love.' It ended bad."

John Marnane turned away with a sigh from this iron code of manners. He had a sense of his own weakness in desiring that strange foreign commodity known as love, and he was not minded to discover it to Peggy's sharp eyes. He lit his candle and went to bed.

Years of inaction had, perhaps, left him with a surplus of energy. Anyhow, he put his old house into the hands of the painter and paper-hanger in the little country town with amazing rapidity. His investments at the auction were stored in an outhouse till the rooms should be ready for them. He displayed a quite unexpected frivolity in the choice of paint and paper. The flowers and the colors were of the gayest. From the mart, as the country town called its big shop, he carried home surreptitiously bundles of flowery chintz and lace curtains and such fripperies.

It must not be supposed that these things did not make a nine days' wonder. The doing-up of John's house took time. He chafed in silence over the slowness of the men, but outwardly he was an image of patient contentment. People stopped him in the road to ply him with questions and chaff. He baffled them clumsily but effectually. They approached old Peg whenever they got an opportunity, but she knew as little as they. The work went on. At last the best bedroom was finished, and John, who had carried himself stolidly before the workmen, was at liberty to moon in and out of the room and admire its beauties beheld of no man.

He had made no attempt to see the girl who had so captivated his fancy. When he had the place ready for her he would ask her. It never occurred to him that she might refuse. He was a "strong" farmer, far wealthier than people thought him, and she was a poor cottager's daughter. He glowed with delight at the thought of the benefits he would bestow upon her.

At last the workmen were finished. John Marnane was leaning over his gate the same evening thinking upon how he should approach the girl. Why he didn't even know her name, and yet his house stood ready for her. He could not much longer restrain the ardor which burned within him. To-morrow he would climb the mountain over there and find her.

As he stood smoking his pipe, to all appearance placidly, Larry Brophy came down the road. The two men nodded.

"When is the haulin' home to be?" asked the newcomer. The curiosity and the jokes were rather stale, and he spoke in a bored voice.

"Very soon, now, Larry," announced John Marnane, and the other man couldn't tell whether he jested or not.

"The house is finished, I hear. I met Fogarty's men going home wid the ladders on a cart."

"It is."

"It'll look well when the sticks is in."

"Well enough," said the owner, with secret pride.

"Got the wardrobe in yet, John?"

"Not yet."

"'Twill be a terrible job to get it in, and up your stairs. You got it chape, but I don't know that it'll be a bargain after all. You'd better have let it fall to Susie Kavanagh, though where she'd put it bangs me."

John's eyes lit up.

"I don't know Susie Kavanagh," he said slowly.

"Kavanagh's daughter that lives in the glen above there. They call her the Cluster of Nuts.

Where wor your eyes, man, not to see the purty face of her?"

"I half disremember," said John, hypocritically. "Was she a stout woman wid a Paisley shawl?"

Larry snorted contemptuously.

"You an' your stout woman! She was a little brown girl wid a frock the color of her cheeks, an' roguish eyes. You ould omadaun, not to have noticed the purtiest girl in the country!"

John laughed delightedly.

"Is it an ould bachelor like me?" he said, expecting a shower of raillery.

"Just as well," went on Larry soberly, "for she was called the third time last Sunday. Young Fenlon's her match. There won't be as handsome a pair to dance at the weddin'."

The other man stared at him with eyes that leaped out of his face. A cold sweat gathered upon his forehead, and a mist before his eyes.

"Well, I must be goin'," said Larry, who had noticed nothing. "Good-evenin' kindly. You'll be sure to ask me to the weddin', John?"

"Oh, aye," said John mechanically.

He went up-stairs to the best bedroom, and sat down on the bedstead, which had been freshly varnished. He looked round the room stupidly, and the blood seemed to come into his eyes. Then an ache of pity for himself smote him dully. He had hoped for a thing for the first and only time in his life, and he had been disappointed. He knew that there would be no spring in him to make him begin anew. His eyes filled with tears, and he began to cry. Again and again, like a great loutish boy, he wiped away the tears with the dirty sleeve of his coat, till he looked more than ever a pitiable object.

It was long before the fountain of his tears was dried. Then at last he lifted his head, and gazed with inflamed eyes at a patch of moonlight on the floor. He spoke out his latest thought in words.

"I'm thinkin'," he said, "that I might as well break up the ould wardrobe wid a hammer."

www.ingramcontent.com/pod-product-compliance
Lightning Source LLC
Chambersburg PA
CBHW031857220426
43663CB00006B/661